PHYLLIS ZAGANO

SACRED
SILENCE

DAILY
MEDITATIONS
FOR LENT

Franciscan
MEDIA
Cincinnati, Ohio

Scripture passages have been taken from *New Revised Standard Version Bible,* copyright ©1989 by the Division of Christian Education of the National Council of the Churches of Christ in the U.S.A., and used by permission. All rights reserved.

Cover and book design by Mark Sullivan
Cover image © PhotoXpress | Mikko Pitkänen

LIBRARY OF CONGRESS CATALOGING-IN-PUBLICATION DATA
Zagano, Phyllis.
Sacred silence : daily meditations for Lent / Phyllis Zagano.
pages cm
ISBN 978-1-61636-718-3 (alk. paper)
1. Lent—Prayers and devotions. 2. Spiritual life—Catholic church. 3.
Silence—Religious aspects—Catholic Church. I. Title.
BX2170.L4Z34 2014
242'.34—dc23
2014033860
ISBN 978-1-61636-718-6

Published by Franciscan Media
28 W. Liberty St.
Cincinnati, OH 45202
www.FranciscanMedia.org

Printed in the United States of America.
Printed on acid-free paper.
14 15 16 17 18   5 4 3 2 1

To the memory of
Peter J. Houle

Be still, and know that I am God.

—Psalm 46:10

CONTENTS

INTRODUCTION

In his Lenten message for 2014, Pope Francis focused on our common humanity, our common hungers, and our common needs for spiritual fulfillment. He wrote that we all face three types of hungers: material (poverty), moral (sin), and spiritual (lack of a relationship with God). Each can be healed with the Gospel but first, Francis wrote, we must be "converted to justice, equality, simplicity and sharing."

We are all hungry. We are destitute and desolate in our search for what will fill us. We usually know what we want; too often we do not know what we need. Do we want fortune? Do we want fame? Do we want a better car or a better house? Do we want more friends or fewer responsibilities?

These are questions of human life. Some are, or at least become, very real needs. Others are merely distracting temptations.

The one thing we really do need is to answer them. We need to pay attention to and select among the great kaleidoscope of choices life puts before us in such a way as to fulfill our legitimate desires without disrupting our own or others' lives. We are always choosing between and among goods, but like the little girl in the toy store whose mother says she can choose just one doll, eventually we need to kiss the other choices good-bye.

So, how do we figure out what we truly need? How do we figure out, therefore, what we really want?

I think we find an answer in silence. Not *the* answer—at least not immediately—but at least the method, the path we can take (each of us) toward the way to find the answer for ourselves, and for no one else.

It is about prayer. It is about stillness. It is about stillness and silence in Lent.

In many parts of the world, Lent begins in the silent time of the year. The earth is gently awakening from its winter slumber, gradually bringing forth its remembered fullness. In other parts of the world, Lent is a time of slowing down, of increasing coolness, of moving toward the dark bright of longer nights, when the burst of dawn truly does break forth day after day, promising more, promising deeper, promising a greater silence and, conversely, promising a greater light.

These are the days we cherish in silence as we move toward the resurrection.

ASH WEDNESDAY
Entering into Silence
JOEL 2:12–18; 2 CORINTHIANS 5:20—6:2; MATTHEW 6:1–6, 16–18

> Yet even now, says the LORD,
>> return to me with all your heart,
> Return to the LORD, your God.
>
> Joel 2:12, 13

L ent is not an intellectual exercise, but an affair of the heart. Ash Wednesday comes around each year. We get ashes. We remember prayer, fasting, and almsgiving. We say we'll do better at something, or not do something else at all. Whatever sin or addiction has plagued us since the turn of the year, the one we have not yet managed to get rid of despite our New Year's resolution to somehow dislodge it at the roots, Lent presents us with another chance. But how?

We think and we think and we plot and we plan. If the use of too much Internet or salt or sleep is on our minds, like the three little pigs we huff and we puff until we blow those little houses down, unfortunately to no avail. We work away at our dependencies as if everything depends on us. It does not. Everything depends on our own dependence on God. And we cannot learn anything about that dependence by thinking and plotting and planning—by huffing and puffing.

We need to open our hearts. We need to be quiet.

But how?

Some time ago, when I was relearning how to pray for the umpteenth time, I realized that I was just plain talking too much. Everything was going on in my head. That was it. Just in my head, nowhere else. I'd built a wall between me and my emotions, a very practical thing to do if you want to maintain control over everything in life. It is not a very practical way to approach prayer, because it stifles the longings of the heart. I yearned for knowledge that I was really praying, that I was someway somehow connecting to the God I said I loved and who I said, at least, I wanted to follow in the way Jesus taught.

But, as I learned in graduate school, so long as I was talking—in graduate school in class or on an oral exam—there was no way I would be questioned, especially no way I would be asked a question I could not answer.

That may work in graduate school, but it is not a smart way to pray.

So here is what I have learned. Take it, or not, as you begin your own journey through Lent. Whether the ground around you is getting colder or warmer, whether the light outside is getting dimmer or brighter, I offer you the suggestion, at least, that the desire you carry in your own heart to listen to and love the Lord with all you are and have will be opened and answered if you offer first of all your own silence to the project.

That does not mean becoming a vegetable. There are many ways of being silent, and many aids to doing so. Of course, if you know what keeps your mind active on thoughts other than the thought of the presence of

God, you should be able to become aware of when such thought presents itself. I hesitate to call whatever it is a "temptation," for it may or may not be. But there are some things in our lives—food, music, conversations— that stick a little more firmly to the surface of our minds and form a sort of coating that keeps away the silence.

I am not saying you need to give up all conversations, or music, and certainly not all food for Lent. I am saying that as we become more and more aware of our need for silence, even throughout this holy season, one or some of these might pop up as a bit of a barrier to silence, and therefore as a bit of a barrier to our maintaining the type of silence we need so as to be able to hear the voice of God in our hearts.

Let me give you an example. I happen to like jazz. I kid around some-times calling it my "liturgical music" because the syncopation and the words of some of the songs, especially the love songs, often fit my mood when I am trying to be alone at prayer. But sometimes, that very syncopa-tion and those very words become an obstacle as they take over my mind. I think here of what is called "the Bolero effect," the repetitive beating of a single strand of music that the French composer Maurice Ravel did on purpose. As the syncopation and words take over my mind, I find I am helpless to hear anything God might present or even to say anything to the Lord. So, sometimes—actually more than sometimes—I "give up" jazz.

Now, there is nothing wrong with jazz. For other people, for other people's minds, the same thing might happen with Gregorian chant, or with ABBA, or with the music of the Beatles. These are all wonderful creations, but they can each in their own way become distractions to the project at hand. Which is silence with an open heart. Which is silence with an open heart before the Lord.

A GRACE FOR TODAY

Lord, give me the courage to open my heart to you in silence.

THURSDAY AFTER ASH WEDNESDAY
Recognizing the Cross
DEUTERONOMY 30:15–20; LUKE 9:22–25

Then he said to them all, "If any want to become my followers, let them deny themselves and take up their cross daily and follow me. For those who want to save their life will lose it, and those who lose their life for my sake will save it."

Luke 9:23–24

The problem with silence is that it can be terrifying. Also, sometimes we mistake loneliness for holy silence before the Lord. It is not. Silence is not loneliness, although we can be silent before the Lord when we are lonely and we can be lonely when we are silent before the Lord.

The big thing we need to recognize is that loneliness is part of the cross of being human. So we recognize it and its pain when it comes, and we ask for the grace to bear it. We are social creatures. We need the comfort of community, of family, and of friends. We need the activity of work, whether inside or outside the house, to participate in the wonderful adventure of life with all around us. But we also need to be alone and silent before God if we are to hold and recognize our own cross, because when we do so we are then able to go back out of solitude to community, to family, and to friends and recognize their crosses, too.

The kind of aloneness that makes us lonely is deliberately choosing not to be near anyone: community, family, or friends, just so we can be alone with ourselves for our own selfish purposes. That is a silly solitude, and it happens to be quite destructive. When someone talks about "blessed solitude—all alone with myself," he or she may have an admiring audience, but only because he or she is looking in a mirror, not at the cross. And looking at the cross is the real project of Lent.

The mystery of the cross is the mystery of self-denial. One of the first things we must deny is ourselves, and the first point in denying ourselves is denying ourselves the comfort of our own self-directed thoughts and daydreams that can masquerade as prayer. We need to avoid any sort of cotton-candy "prayer" that goes nowhere and does nothing. So, what to do?

When we are totally self-focused, when all our prayer is always and only a recitation of our own woes, it's time to chat with someone who can help us break the self-feeding cycle. Yes, we lay everything at the foot of the cross—every sorrow and every joy—and in so doing maintain the face of Jesus before us always. We need to take up our crosses, but we also need to be gentle with them and with ourselves. If we sit holding our own crosses too tightly we will not be able to put our arms around anyone else, nor will they be able to put their arms around us. That includes God.

A GRACE FOR TODAY

Lord, help me to know that my life is at your disposal.

FRIDAY AFTER ASH WEDNESDAY
Understanding Fasting
ISAIAH 58:1–9A; MATTHEW 9:14–15

> Jesus said to them, "The wedding guests cannot mourn
> as long as the bridegroom is with them, can they? The
> days will come when the bridegroom is taken away from
> them, and then they will fast."
>
> Matthew 9:15

Lent is a time for fasting. The question in today's Gospel is: Why don't Jesus's disciples fast? The answer is that his teaching calls for a different kind of fasting.

Sometimes we get confused about fasting. We think it is only negative—don't do this, don't eat that. Yet, there is a positive fasting that can be genuinely beneficial and can enrich our Lenten journey.

How? Well, what kinds of things do we usually fast from? You know the list. But, what kinds of things *should* we fast from? The first thing that comes to my mind is negative thoughts, the thoughts that dive into our minds and brains and even stomachs: I did this, I did not do this. I am not talking about ignoring wrongful actions here—of course we need to fast from them. I am talking about fasting from the negative thinking that twists us into neurotic spasms of self-loathing.

When you think of it, there are many ways of fasting. The usual are fine: no sweets, no late nights, no bad language. But each of these can be driven by an indulgent self-help motivation. Building a "better me" is fine, so long as we understand the purpose of that "better me." If we connect our fasting to the call to a deep and personal participation in the human project—to be a part of the community, whether large or small, personal or impersonal—we are on the right track. That is how we measure our fasting.

Sometimes fasting means fasting from spending time on my own projects. Then the time I reserved for my personal whatever, I can reserve instead as gift for my community, large or small. That may mean taking a trip to the museum with an aging parent, or spending just a little more time with a friend in need, or running a small parish project for the local food bank. Such fasting will not get me through the latest clothing catalogue or crossword puzzle, and I may miss a favorite television program, but this gift of time connects me to another or to others. And that is what the Christian project is all about.

It is when we do not have any connection to others, when we are so wrapped up in our own preferred solitude, alone and undisturbed, that we distance ourselves from the living Christ in our midst. That is the wrong kind of fasting. It is not the silence of the contemplative, but the silence of the selfish.

Of course, we do not need to be constantly in the company of others, and for many of us the actual connection with others is extremely difficult. But every one of us can do as the American champion of the poor,

Dorothy Day, did and carry with us lists of people and events to pray for. If we are really all out of ideas, all we need to do is check the morning's news. Someone will be suffering.

Life is not always happy, but our connections to others can create a simple and grace-filled quiet celebration of our own and others' lives. These others are the presence of Christ in our lives. To be sure, everybody likes a good party. Jesus says that so long as the bridegroom is around, the party is on, and we can and must celebrate every one of these others.

A GRACE FOR TODAY
Lord, help me know what to fast from.

SATURDAY AFTER ASH WEDNESDAY
Healing
ISAIAH 58:9B–14; LUKE 5:27–32

After this he went out and saw a tax collector named
Levi, sitting at the tax booth; and he said to him, "Follow
me." And he got up, left everything, and followed him.

Luke 5:27–28

The Church, Pope Francis once said, is a "field hospital for the wounded." And we are all wounded; we are all in need of healing.

When Jesus stopped by the customs post and saw Levi—we know this disciple as Matthew—Jesus called him. That is a pretty startling thing in and of itself. Here is someone with one of the most despised professions in the world, and Jesus chooses him. In the world of Jesus's time a tax collector was even more despised than today. That is because most, if not all, ancient tax collectors made a profit, a big profit, on what they collected. If they were changing money, they took a cut. If they were noting taxes, they took a cut. If they were dishonest, they took a cut. One way or another, they made their profit. One way or another, the poor taxpayer lost out.

So for Jesus to call Levi is a pretty startling thing in and of itself, but it is even more startling that Jesus ended up at this tax collector's home with a crowd of other tax collectors, and at a banquet besides! For Jesus to eat with these men (and we can assume in Jesus's time they were all men) is nearly a scandal, and the Pharisees and scribes point that out. "Why do you eat and drink with tax collectors and sinners?" they ask.

Jesus gives his answer: Those "who are well do not need a physician, but those who are sick." What can this mean?

The first thing I think of, using Pope Francis's analogy of the field hospital, is that Jesus sees himself not at a party with a bunch of thieves, but rather as walking into the medical tent of war where the wounded are all around him. Their wounds are obvious to him: gluttony and greed; probably pride and sloth; perhaps lust, anger, and envy. Each of these wounds, whether major of minor in any individual soul, must be tended to and healed.

The triage of the soul that we all need cannot be done alone. The identification of what wounds are most serious and in need of repair can only happen with deep humility when we speak to another about our lives. There are many ways to seek this healing. Spiritual direction and the sacramental practice of confession are time-honored means of addressing our self-inflicted wounds, wounds that keep us at a distance from others and, actually, from ourselves.

There are other wounds that God can heal, and will heal—the wounds of daily life. But, the beginning of real healing is with the kinds of wounds the scribes and Pharisees saw so well in that crowd at Levi's table with Jesus. We need to remember that our task is not to judge, but to help heal.

That could mean a mother's gentle correction of a child, or the understanding ear and heart of the professional minister. That could mean as well not judging ourselves, but rather looking for and accepting God's healing touch, no matter how it comes to us.

A GRACE FOR TODAY

Lord, help me recognize and accept your healing.

FIRST SUNDAY OF LENT
Starting and Stopping

Year A: Genesis 2:7–9, 3:1–7; Romans 5:12–19; Matthew 4:1–11
Year B: Genesis 9:8–15; 1 Peter 3:18–22; Mark 1:12–15
Year C: Deuteronomy 26:4–10; Romans 10:8–13; Luke 4:1–13

> Then Jesus was led up by the Spirit into the wilderness
> to be tempted by the devil. He fasted forty days and forty
> nights, and afterwards he was famished. The tempter
> came and said to him, "If you are the Son of God, command
> these stones to become loaves of bread."
>
> Matthew 4:1–3

Here it is, the first Sunday of Lent, and even though we have a long way to go, already we are tired. There are so many other things that grasp our attention: riches, honor, pride. Prayer cannot be a priority, because we have to do, see, hear, taste, touch, or smell something else. Besides, the desert of Lent is dark, silent, tasteless, lonely, and often foul-smelling.

But wait a minute. Who led us into this desert? For Jesus in the Gospel, it was the Spirit, and in fact that is the case for us as well. So for us to be in this desert of Lent, to actually spend the time on our Lenten pursuits (whatever they may be) we need to remember who got us here, and why.

That will pull us through any starting and stopping, any falling and failing, any disheartening days when we say it is just too hard to continue.

There will always be temptations. I think of the trio of riches-honor-pride as the temptations against what the Church has come to call the evangelical counsels of poverty, chastity, and obedience that men and women religious vow themselves to live. When you think of it, we are all called to these.

We are naturally attracted to riches. But how we obtain them and how we relate to them are key to our ongoing growth as Christians. Stealing and hoarding are the gross examples. Minor cheating and withholding more than we need from others are the more subtle ways our attraction to riches can work its way into our psyches.

It is the same with honor. We all have the appetite for honors. We enjoy the accolades of others, the recognition and the applause. But our appetites can feed our own destruction, especially our appetites for comfort and for sex. We are all called to chastity in our chosen states of life. What that means, personally, individually, is within the province of prayer.

And so too with pride. An overwhelming undercurrent of pride can mar every desert experience and every life. Yet we are called to obedience, again to obedience to the way God has loved us into being. Genuine obedience, of course, does not mean someone else's lock-step control of every aspect of our lives. But it does mean being aware of and available to the people in our lives in a coordinated fashion that reverences us and them as well.

The Tempter can approach us in each of these areas, can sway us one way or the other to riches, to honor, to pride. The simplest thing to do is to receive and accept that fact of our humanity gratefully and gracefully. We make mistakes. We forget. We get tired. But it is the Spirit who is leading us through this desert and the Spirit who remains with us there.

A GRACE FOR TODAY

Lord, let me not fear temptation.

MONDAY OF THE FIRST WEEK OF LENT
Who Is Jesus?
LEVITICUS 19:1–2, 11–18; MATTHEW 25:31–46

Truly I tell you, just as you did it to one of the least of
these who are members of my family, you did it to me.

Matthew 25:40

The twenty-fifth chapter of Matthew's Gospel has lots of practical advice. Here, Jesus explains how to find him. It is not that complicated.

If we feed the hungry, give drink to the thirsty, welcome the stranger, clothe the naked, and visit the imprisoned, we have made a good start in locating Jesus in our midst. But first we need to recognize Jesus.

I made a long retreat once, and spent many days at and around a retreat house on the shore. There were houses—very big houses—around, but most of my days were spent out of sight of others, either in my room or on the small and empty beach in front of the house. I saw very few people, except at Mass and meals. Even then, except when I spoke with my director, I was not really looking at the others I passed or sat next to, and I rarely, if ever, looked into their eyes.

Toward the end of the retreat I needed to see Jesus, by which I mean I needed to actually look at other people. So I went to the mall.

If that sounds strange, hear me out. When we tend to the needs of Jesus in our own lives, we are tending to the needs of others, whether strangers or persons in our smaller or larger circles or communities. I needed to look into the eyes of Jesus. I needed to see the middle-aged woman pushing her father along in a wheelchair. I needed to see the young family with the two little girls trying on pink scarves. I needed to see the man considering, very carefully, a power drill. I needed to know that each and every one of these people was the Christ I say I want to tend to, to pray for, to speak and to write for.

You are the same. There are times when we need to be alone with God in prayerful solitude, but if we maintain a stillness and a silence throughout our daily lives (by which I mean not abusing our senses) then we will be drawn out of ourselves to a loving and compassionate look at all around us.

That stillness and silence will allow us to recognize our own hunger, thirst, aloneness, embarrassment, and imprisonment. When we recognize the wounded Jesus in ourselves, we are quite likely to go out of our hearts and minds to recognize him in those around us. And, as we tend our own selves, we are moved to tend others as we can, whether directly through action or indirectly through prayer. Our lives can truly echo the caring words and provide the caring touch of Christ.

A GRACE FOR TODAY

Lord, help me see you in others.

TUESDAY OF THE FIRST WEEK OF LENT
How to Pray
ISAIAH 55:10–11; MATTHEW 6:7–15

When you are praying, do not heap up empty phrases as
the Gentiles do; for they think that they will be heard
because of their many words. Do not be like them, for
your Father knows what you need before you ask him.

Matthew 6:7–8

We tend to forget that Jesus's disciples had a long upward climb to
figure out who he was and what he was about. They knew they
were deeply and personally attracted to him. But, beyond that, there was
lots of learning to go on before they could be sent out to cure, to heal, to
preach, and to teach. So, one of the first things Jesus did for the disciples
was to sit them down and talk to them about prayer.

There are many ways of praying. Wise people often say: Pray as you can,
not as you cannot. Here Jesus is presenting the simple axiom that is really
a quite stunning lesson. We do not need to pile up words upon words in
order to be heard in the heart of God. Jesus also has a very comforting
message: The Father knows what we need even before we ask for it.

Today's complete Gospel reading repeats what is known as the Lord's
Prayer or the Our Father, a prayer shared by over two billion Christians
that has similarities to earlier Jewish prayers of dependence on God. When

we say this prayer, we acknowledge the fact that we are human, that we are created in God's graced and loving care as individuals with free will to make choices in our lives.

This does not mean we should be free agents acting on our own behalf without thought of others. What it does mean is that we are creatures who can choose and, when we choose rightly in accord with God's loving creation of us, we can live in accord with his will. As a matter of fact, the Our Father we say so easily is truly a pledge of dependence on God and God's will. If we see God in all things, we can better understand what Jesus is teaching us to say.

We also need to remember that Jesus is teaching us that we do not have to say much. God knows what we need. So, when we think of the four basic ways of praying—adoration, contrition, petition, thanksgiving—we will remember that each one has an element of silence. We sit in adoration of the wonder and wonders of God; we know the sadness in contrition for our wrong acts; we understand God's care as we think about what we need; we smile in gratitude at the many gifts within and without our very selves.

Of all the words of prayer I've read about or heard or said, the most powerful are contained in the simple phrase "Thank you." These, to me, are the basis of prayer, and actually the basis of the Our Father and any prayer we may have learned. So, maybe today it would be a good idea to take Jesus's words to heart. Say the Our Father. Say, "Thank you."

A GRACE FOR TODAY

Lord, teach me to pray.

WEDNESDAY OF THE FIRST WEEK OF LENT
Signs and Signals
JONAH 3:1–10; LUKE 11:29–32

> When the crowds were increasing, he began to say, "This
> generation is an evil generation; it asks for a sign, but no
> sign will be given to it except the sign of Jonah. For just
> as Jonah became a sign to the people of Nineveh, so the
> Son of Man will be to this generation."
>
> Luke 11:29–30

Nineveh was once the greatest city of the world. Like London, Tokyo, and New York, it was a center of wealth and power. Scripture tells us the city fell to the many temptations of greatness and began a long, slow slide of self-destruction. Jonah, who endured his own difficult darkness, became a sign and preached repentance to the Ninevites. Because of his preaching they repented.

Preaching repentance—successfully—is not an easy task. Changing some of the ways of the world, whether in London, Tokyo, New York, or in your own hometown, is not something for the faint of heart. Surely, the entire populations of cities and towns are not evil, but there is evil masquerading as good in each one of them. Evil floats along in fashion, in industry, in entertainment, and in commerce. Each in its own way offers evil the opportunity to take root and to grow.

We must also add to the difficulty of confronting evil the complication that societies always like to be affirmed in their beliefs. The preference to be affirmed in evil beliefs lives on in societies both large and small. In a family, small misunderstandings can fester into deep anger. In a community, a little slander can go a long way, as cliques form, gossip multiplies, people are damaged. In work environments, small events of graft or other financial corruption slither along unnoticed for decades. Whether in the family, the community, or at work, we can mistake the glint of evil for a good.

We are not innately evil, but we are naturally always choosing what we see as good. And evil has a funny way of presenting itself attractively. There is nothing new about the fact of evil attempting to enter human hearts. Jesus, now over two thousand years ago, preached, "this generation is an evil generation." Why?

The fact of the matter is every generation can be an evil generation of sorts. Our contemporary evils—the things that turn us away from our own humanity—are no different from those of earlier generations. Now, however, many evils move more quickly through electronic media of communication. We see more of evils presented as good, through bad cinema and art. We hear more of evils that hurt populations and the environment. We even speak more of evils. How can we not? Dictators starve populations, corporations damage the environment, and individuals corrupt the innocent.

We want to see our personal understandings of faith and morals triumph, but two-thirds of the world does not recognize Jesus as Son of God, any more than the people of an earlier age recognized Jonah. Others' religious beliefs are not the problem. Evil is. Let us be attentive to the enticements of evil.

A GRACE FOR TODAY

Lord, help me resist the worldly denial of good.

THURSDAY OF THE FIRST WEEK OF LENT
Asking for Help
ESTHER C: 12, 14–16, 23–25; MATTHEW 7:7–12

Ask, and it will be given you; search, and you will find; knock, and the door will be opened for you. For everyone who asks receives, and everyone who searches finds, and for everyone who knocks, the door will be opened.

Matthew 7:7–8

Sometimes when I think about how evil works, in the world and in my life, I think of myself walking through a sandstorm. The winds whistle and blown sand surrounds me. Sometimes it stings my eyes, so I hold them shut fast. Mostly I keep walking, but I just cannot see and I lose my way.

One of evil's more subtle tricks is to suggest that I do not need any help in finding my way. "You can read maps," it whispers in your ear. "You do not need any help. You've done that before. You have outgrown the need for...." Here your own mind actually provides the end of the sentence. Perhaps you have been helped by a confessor, or by a spiritual director, or by an older sibling, or by a teacher, or mentor, or friend. You can be sure that evil will be only too happy to convince you that (1) the help was incorrect, and you should ignore it; (2) you are a big kid now, and have no need to ask anyone anything; and, perhaps evil's favorite, (3) you are no longer a sinner so just forget all that confession and spiritual direction business.

Well, guess what? We all need a little help getting on in this life. There is no way to go it alone. The trouble is, once you accept that, things can get harder, not easier. Where to go? Whom to ask? Well, we can all start by asking the Lord. Sifting through the day's activities in God's presence each evening is a good thing to do. Here we can notice our feelings. Here we can notice how we reacted to one or another event or person. Here, also, we can see where we might need a little help. Finally, here we can spend a little time considering just who might be of help. And, if no one comes to mind, perhaps this alone is an item for prayer.

We are so used to asking for things in prayer—in the comforting prayer of petition—but we sometimes cannot put on finger on exactly what it is we want. So, in today's Gospel we are encouraged to ask for what we want, even if we are not exactly positively sure what it is. If we seek, what exactly will we find? If we knock, what exactly will be behind the opened door?

It is often a good thing just to ask in the silent prayer of our hearts for what God wants for us, for how God will guide us through the blinding sandstorm of life, for God perhaps to suggest someone to help. No matter if there are no immediate answers. The important thing is to keep asking. Evil suggests that persistence is mere stubbornness, but common sense reminds us we need to pay attention to our needs.

A GRACE FOR TODAY

Lord, let me understand the kind of help I need.

FRIDAY OF THE FIRST WEEK OF LENT
Making Peace
EZEKIEL 18:21–28; MATTHEW 5:20–26

So when you are offering your gift at the altar, if you remember that your brother or sister has something against you, leave your gift there before the altar and go; first be reconciled to your brother or sister, and then come and offer your gift.

Matthew 5:23–24

There is no sense in trying to ignore anger when we pray. When that anger is directed at another person, we really have two things we need to do: First, we must try to make peace if we can. Second, whether we can or cannot make peace, we must also forgive the other in the stillness of our hearts. Forgiving is not forgetting, so when we have been wronged we do not need to think it was all our fault. It does, however, take two to create an argument, so there may be something in there for you to blame yourself for. And, sometimes there is no way we can reconcile the wrongs we have suffered, but interior peace can come from praying for those who have wounded us.

Of course sometimes we have wounded ourselves. The hurt and the anger we create in our own hearts is the bloom of tiny seeds of sin. If we refuse to free an imprisoned memory of contention—and in this Gospel we are reminded that someone might have something against us, for which we must apologize—we will lock ourselves into a very uncomfortable space.

The important thing here is asking for forgiveness, surely from God, but often through the sacramental ministry of a priest. God knows and forgives even before we ask, and through the ministry of the priest we enjoy the forgiveness of the whole Church. I often think the real import of confession is that through its practice we are recognizing what blinded us in the first place. No matter what it is, whether relatives of anger or sloth or lust or any other slimy thing that may be creeping around in our lives, we need to sit quietly and recognize where and how we give this particular fault house room. Then we need to mention this to another person. Often we need to mention this in sacramental confession.

But, sometimes we do not. There is an ancient practice in the Church known as spiritual direction, where you sit with another person and talk about the way your heart beats in relation to God, to yourself, and to others in your life. Sometimes things in these discussions touch on sin, but unlike sacramental confession, sin or sinful acts are not the focus. Rather, the focus is on how you let yourself be distanced, how you refused to let yourself be at peace with the world around you and what it holds for you. The focus is on actually being God's beautiful creation.

The bottom line in reconciliation is really at the top of the list: reconciliation with yourself. As you grow in God's care, that peace will bring you peace, even with your adversaries.

A GRACE FOR TODAY

Lord, help me make peace with myself and others.

SATURDAY OF THE FIRST WEEK OF LENT
Loving Others
DEUTERONOMY 26:16–19; MATTHEW 5:43–48

I say to you, Love your enemies and pray for those who persecute you, so that you may be children of your Father in heaven; for he makes his sun rise on the evil and on the good, and sends rain on the righteous and on the unrighteous.

Matthew 5:44–45

There is nothing more destructive than carrying a grudge throughout life. It is like a sack of rocks that only gets heavier, mainly because we keep adding to it. Yet, we insist on carrying all those rocks around. We even insist on picking up a few pebbles or stones from our memories along the way, adding to the burden of anger that weighs us down.

I have been that way. Like the rest of humanity, I have been wronged, sometimes by people I trusted and respected. I am not talking about being cut off on the highway by a stranger, or suffering a smart remark from a colleague in the parking lot. Like you, there are positions I thought I should have gotten, into which I put an extraordinary amount of time and effort, all of which came to naught.

But did it? Did my seeking what I eventually could not have really cause that much difficulty in my life? Or did I cause my own difficulty by not letting go of the experience and by not accepting the results?

If I place the cast of characters in my mind for any of the many times I have been wronged, or have been treated unfairly, I would literally need more room! Then what happens? I simply have no room in my mind for anything else. The event or incident plays and replays like the repetitive call of the cuckoo bird, not stopping and certainly not giving me any peace. If I hang on to these old memories, and replay them like old movies in my mind, I will create in myself the same feelings I had when I was first wronged. To be sure, there are instances in my life and in yours when we have been genuinely wronged. But to replay the scenario over and over does nothing but dig the hurt deeper and deeper into the psyche.

I am not suggesting you just forget about everything. I am suggesting, along with today's Gospel, that one way to lessen the pain is to pray for those who have hurt you. That does not mean bringing them to mind every minute of the day. What is does mean is to place them in God's care when they do appear in your thoughts, even if it happens to be every minute of the day.

It is easy to love distant enemies. We love to think how good we are when we pray for the opponent in war or in politics. That, of course, is the trap of pride, and it can deflect us from the real things we need to bring to God in prayer. It is a great deal more difficult to love the one who has hurt us. We do not need to excuse wrongs, or even to forget them, but we must always forgive.

Today's readings teach us that we all have the same internal opportunities for peace and happiness. By way of analogy, we are taught that we all have the same sun shining on us and we all have the same rain falling on us. It is how we deal with sun and rain, how we deal with the happy and the not-so-happy things of life that causes our interior weather. Basically, we do it to ourselves.

A GRACE FOR TODAY

Lord, grant me the grace to forgive my enemies.

SECOND SUNDAY OF LENT
Keep Moving

YEAR A: GENESIS 12:1–4A; 2 TIMOTHY 1:8–10; MATTHEW 17:1–9

YEAR B: GENESIS 22:1–2, 9A, 10–13, 15–18;

ROMANS 8:31B–34; MARK 9:2–10

YEAR C: GENESIS 15:5–12, 17–18; PHILIPPIANS 3:17—4:1;

LUKE 9:28B–36

And while he was praying, the appearance of his face
changed, and his clothes became dazzling white. Just as
they were leaving him, Peter said to Jesus, "Master, it is
good for us to be here; let us make three dwellings, one
for you, one for Moses, and one for Elijah"—not knowing
what he said.

Luke-9:29, 33

When something wonderful happens we want to "build three tents"
and just stay where we are. There is nothing better than staying in
good times, in peace, and in calm. Of course, God wants us to enjoy life,
but we cannot stop at one event. I know well the temptation to stay in one
place, but when you think about it, staying in one place is no way to grow.
It is especially no way to grow in God's grace.

The ongoing challenge of the Gospel is to keep moving, and to keep moving forward. We know not to get stuck in old arguments and hurts, replaying them over and over in our minds as if they were Academy Award-winning movies. There is nothing wrong with working on these issues, especially with working on these issues with help from competent people, but we cannot let them take over our entire lives. Lent is a time of purgation, a time of freeing ourselves from the big and little things that bind us. We usually think of these as the negative things in our lives, but the positive memories can bind us equally strongly.

For example, if we have had wonderfully positive experiences in life, whether in school or in work, we can hang on to these memories at the expense of living in the present. So, we don't make new friends. We don't go out of ourselves to enjoy new experiences. We end up, eventually, hating where we are because we are no longer where we were. Our minds get clogged with wishing for the past, when the fact of the matter is that living in the present and looking forward to the future is the way to go.

When we sit in the face of the reality of God's grace—and at this point in Lent it is good to recall the Transfiguration—we have the opportunity to realize that the present is what we need to concentrate on, and that the future is what we can look forward to. When Jesus appeared transfigured before the apostles there on the mountain, he was showing them and us who he is now and who he is in our, and his, eternal futures. That is the promise of the Gospel. That is the promise of a life in Christ.

Bottom line: The overwhelming beauty of the Transfiguration the apostles enjoyed prefigures our own participation in the resurrection. But that overwhelming beauty is God's pledge and promise to us only if we keep moving. We keep moving by repairing the hurts of our past as best we can, by savoring the happy memories in those same pasts, and by recognizing that all we have for sure is the present; all we have for sure is the now.

A GRACE FOR TODAY

Lord, help me to enter fully, joyfully, into the present.

MONDAY OF THE SECOND WEEK OF LENT
Judging and Being Judged
Daniel 9:4b–10; Luke 6:36–38

Be merciful, just as your Father is merciful.

Do not judge, and you will not be judged; do not condemn, and you will not be condemned. Forgive, and you will be forgiven; give, and it will be given to you. A good measure, pressed down, shaken together, running over, will be put into your lap; for the measure you give will be the measure you get back.

Luke 6:36–38

Today's image is of God the shopkeeper, sifting flour, measuring it out to overflowing, and packing it down to be sure we get the full amount.

If I think of myself in a marketplace standing there before the merchant, what is my attitude? Am I content, even delighted, with what I receive when the merchant gets to me? Do I leave happy that I have something to give to my friends and family? Or, am I angry if the merchant seems to pay attention to another customer before me? Do I watch carefully to see if he is giving me the full measure? Am I frightened that I will drop or spoil what I eventually do receive?

Such are my choices: trust or not trust, judge or not judge, condemn or not condemn. If we approach life with an open mind and an open heart, we can allow for the wisps of confusion that cross our paths. If not, we can turn into very unhappy complainers.

I remember being in an automobile with a few people leaving a church parking lot. The driver was slightly nervous and driving very slowly—she had not been in this parking lot before—and the driver of another car honked the horn. The driver of the car I was in reacted somewhat angrily; someone else suggested that the honking horn belonged to a person in need of a bathroom. "Oh," the driver said, "I never thought of that." Even if it was not the case, the idea that the horn-honker might have a slight emergency did calm my nervous driver's anger.

That is a simple example, but you have to admit it happens every day. Someone wants to get ahead of us in one way or another, and we become terribly annoyed. I recall the advice the founder of a group of women religious gave his sisters in the nineteenth century: Try to find a charitable explanation for everything. I think that is good advice.

Of course church parking lots are the least of it. We are complex beings, with opportunities to live and grow in God's grace minute by minute, every day. And every day we have the opportunity to be mistrustful, to judge, and to complain.

Jesus teaches us to live honestly and to be merciful. If we do not judge, condemn, or withhold forgiveness, neither will we be judged, condemned, or remain unforgiven. That, to me, is the way to go.

A GRACE FOR TODAY

Lord, help me understand the person who puzzles me.

TUESDAY OF THE SECOND WEEK OF LENT
Humility 101
Isaiah 1:10, 16–20; Matthew 23:1–12

They do all their deeds to be seen by others; for they
make their phylacteries broad and their fringes long.
They love to have the place of honor at banquets and
the best seats in the synagogues, and to be greeted with
respect in the marketplaces, and to have people call
them rabbi.

Matthew 23:5–7

Jesus is pretty clear here talking about the scribes and Pharisees, at least
about the ones who need to make sure everybody else knows they are
better than the rest. Jesus is pretty hard on the rabbis as well.

To put it all in perspective, I think we need to recognize that there are
people in the Church—whether laypersons, religious, or clerics—who are
just plain insufferable. They know, to the last jot and tittle, exactly what is
right and what is wrong and there is no arguing with them. They act as if
they have God's unlisted phone number. You know as well as I do that even
though they make a lot of noise, most people ignore them.

Then there are the real teachers, the ones who hold God's Word in their hearts and freely open themselves to share it. These are the humble teachers, who know they own nothing of their own accord, and whose soft-spoken words hit home. They teach us how to be.

Humility is crucial to the Lenten journey, and it is truly difficult for anyone to be humble. Sometimes we really do know more than the next person. Sometimes we really do know what is correct or more life-giving. But unless it is our job to correct, we do not need to go about fixing everyone and everything. Even when it is our job—we are teachers, or managers, or superiors of one type or another—there are ways and there are ways.

For example, the humble teacher or manager or superior does not need to advertise corrections. He or she gains nothing by correcting or criticizing before others, and consequently embarrassing the student or subordinate or community member. A quiet word is usually enough.

On the smaller and more personal level, we daily face challenges to humility because, let's face it, we like "places of honor at banquets, seats of honor in synagogues, greetings in marketplaces...." And sometimes we get them without asking for them.

I recall being in Rome at an outdoor Mass at St. Peter's Basilica. A friend in the Vatican's bureaucracy gave me a ticket. I arrived early, and found the seat that matched my ticket number in the back row on the top plaza, but still not far from the outdoor papal altar. As the moment of the Mass approached, one of the pope's gentlemen asked me to move a bit forward, which I did. Soon, another papal gentleman moved me even closer to where the cardinals and diplomats would be seated. My friend was seated on the other side, and after the Mass became quite irate that I had abused the invitation by sitting in the wrong section. I tried to explain that the papal gentlemen had moved me up. My friend walked away, ahead of me, barely speaking as we left St. Peter's Square. I don't think that ever got resolved.

What was I to do? Should I have told the pope's gentleman I did not wish to move? Should I have screamed at my friend to defend myself? Or, should I just remain quiet? Unfortunately, sometimes people freeze their opinions of a person or of an event and they just cannot change. They only hear (or believe) what they want. It is hard to accept that, especially when we feel we are wronged, but there are some things you just cannot change. That event ended up being pretty humiliating for me. But it taught me something about humility.

If we try to see everyone and everything through God's eyes with humility, we will begin to accept an attitude of humility in our hearts and we will begin to be humble.

A GRACE FOR TODAY

Lord, teach me humility.

WEDNESDAY OF THE SECOND WEEK OF LENT
Status Symbols
JEREMIAH 18:18–20; MATTHEW 20:17–28

Then the mother of the sons of Zebedee came to him
with her sons, and kneeling before him, she asked a favor
of him. And he said to her, "What do you want?" She said
to him, "Declare that these two sons of mine will sit, one
at your right hand and one at your left, in your kingdom."

Matthew 20:20–21

Here we go again: the seating chart. Everybody needs a good seat. It makes perfect sense for a mother to ask that her sons have preference. However, the underlying beliefs of this passage seem to peek through. Jesus has made it quite clear that his kingdom is not of this world. So, what exactly is the mother of the sons of Zebedee asking for?

Chances are she does not fully grasp Jesus's preaching, any more than perhaps the other apostles, who are grumbling over her request. Places of honor imply status and status brings power, and would not anyone like to have the power of God? Of course. The problem is that many people think they do already!

But there is a confusing recommendation in this Gospel passage. Jesus says, quite plainly, that places of honor are not for his apostles. If they are to be leaders, they will not lord their rule over others, they will not make their authority felt. The one who wishes to be great will be a servant.

Greatness is connected to servitude. That is not the way of the world in Jesus's Palestine. Servants were lower than low, and the more servants you had, the greater you were. There was nothing noteworthy about being a servant, even the loyal servant of a good master.

Jesus says, quite plainly, that places of honor are not for his apostles. If they are to be leaders they will not lord their rule over others, they will not make their authority felt. The one who wishes to be great will be a servant.

"The Servant Song," by New Zealander Richard Gillard, is a beautiful mediation on this passage. I heard it at a liturgy, just at the start of a retreat. I was seated next to my assigned director. The first line asks, "Will you let me be your servant?" and, later, in the third stanza, we hear:

> I will hold the Christ light for you
> In the night time of your fear
> I will hold my hand out to you
> Speak the peace you long to hear.

What encouraging words! Whose voice do we hear in them? For me, it has often been friends or professional ministers. But who else's voice is in these words? I would say it is a good thing to go through life singing this song in at least three-part harmony in every event, the three voices being yours, God's, and the person helping you or whom you are helping. The fact of the matter is that when we help, we are helped. When we serve, we are served.

Jesus's surprise suggestion that his followers—and we—become servants follows on his earlier advice about humility. Can we keep that advice singing in our hearts?

A GRACE FOR TODAY

Lord, let me be a servant.

THURSDAY OF THE SECOND WEEK OF LENT
Listening
JEREMIAH 17:5–10; LUKE 16:19–31

> Abraham replied, "They have Moses and the prophets;
> they should listen to them." He said, "No, father Abraham;
> but if someone goes to them from the dead, they will
> repent." He said to him, "If they do not listen to Moses
> and the prophets, neither will they be convinced even if
> someone rises from the dead."
>
> Luke 16:29–31

We hear so much, but often we listen to nothing, and to no one. Part of this comes from our internal buzz saw that keeps whirring along, working on old problems, new problems, possible problems, half-forgotten problems. Part of this comes from our own unwillingness to be silent, whether with others or when we are alone.

The parable of poor Lazarus applies to nations, organizations, and ourselves, but there are few parts in it that we really want to listen to. Do we really want to hear that if we consume everything and leave nothing for the poor, we will have consumed our rewards as well? Do we really want to hear today's prophetic voices, as they shout to us about the ways we treat the building blocks of life: earth, air, fire, and water?

The earth is our home. The land and sea are all we have to sustain us. Can we stand to listen to the truthful commentary about strip mining or pesticides? The air is all we have to breathe. Can we stand to listen to the truthful commentary about pollution and the ozone layer?

We need heat, the real and metaphorical fire that we use to warm ourselves, our houses, and our food. Are we overusing it? Does our search for too much warmth and comfort ignore the limits of our natural resources?

And we need water. The water we use for recreation we also use for industry. We take the fishes and plant life from the sea for food and fertilizer. We move water from its natural places to make new territories for housing and farming. Will we listen to those who say that water shortages are the next major crisis?

It seems that, like the rich man begging Abraham, we will get the same answer. The world today has its own descendants of Moses who tell of laws. The world has its prophets, who speak out loudly about the ways we are disfiguring the planet.

Are we waiting for the earth to die? It will not rise up again if we kill it.

A GRACE FOR TODAY

Lord, help me quietly learn to love your creation.

FRIDAY OF THE SECOND WEEK OF LENT
Watching and Waiting
GENESIS 37:3–4, 12–13A, 17B–28A; MATTHEW 21:33–43, 45–46

> Jesus said to them, "Have you never read in the scriptures:
> 'The stone that the builders rejected
>   has become the cornerstone;
> this was the Lord's doing,
>   and it is amazing in our eyes'?
> Therefore I tell you, the kingdom of God will be taken
> away from you and given to a people that produces the
> fruits of the kingdom."
>
>   Matthew 21:42–43

The Lenten journey takes a pretty sharp turn with today's readings. Jesus is teaching the crowds with the parable of the rich landowner, whose servants and, finally, whose own son is beaten and killed by the tenants left to care for the vineyard. The tenants' actions are for nothing, because the rich landowner just gets new tenants to care for the vineyard,

Some commentators see Jesus's words in this parable as demonstrating the ways of religion. If you cannot care for the sacred, you will be replaced. The "Kingdom of God will be taken away from you and given to a people that will produce its fruit." Who are these people?

I do not think it is right to say that Jesus is here pointing to one modern religion over another. Nor do I think he is making what would essentially be a political claim. I do think Jesus is warning the people who heard him then, along with the people who try to hear him now, that the world's evil ways—here demonstrated by the actions of the tenants—never bring about good.

Is Jesus the murdered son of the landowner? The chief priests and Pharisees know full well he is talking about them. They are stuck right now, they cannot get rid of him because he has too much of a positive following. The crowds believe Jesus is a prophet.

If you let your heart feel what Jesus must be feeling, you will know the prophet's dismay. Jesus speaks the truth, yet he must know that death is approaching. He has crossed too many lines. He has criticized too many people. In the current expression, he spoke truth to power. But power does not like prophecy.

Like the rich landowner who sent his servants to the vineyard, God first sent prophets, but their world ignored them. Then, God sent his own Son, and his world ignored him. If we sink into the deadly understanding of this parable as it foretells Jesus's death, we will begin to be consumed by the fear of evil as it beats against the good.

Jesus is rejected. Jesus faces the ultimate rejection. In today's Gospel passage, he quotes Psalm 118: The stone rejected by the builders will become the cornerstone. That is true, but it is cold comfort as we look about the world to see how Jesus is rejected each and every day. No matter where we look we see the face of Christ disfigured by war, by famine, by violence.

We know that Jesus's crucifixion is near, and so does Jesus. If we allow ourselves to feel and to feel deeply that sense of fear and dismay, perhaps it will allow us to look beyond this Gospel passage to where it is lived out day after weary day in our own world.

A GRACE FOR TODAY
Lord, let me feel dismay as the world ignores you.

SATURDAY OF THE SECOND WEEK OF LENT
Hope Survives
MICAH 7:14–15, 18–20; LUKE 15:1–3, 11–32

Then the father said to him, "Son, you are always with me, and all that is mine is yours. But we had to celebrate and rejoice, because this brother of yours was dead and has come to life; he was lost and has been found."

Luke 15:31–32

This is a long and complex story. The two sons split up: One went off to see the world, while the other stayed with his father and worked. The one squandered his fortune, while the other stayed close and faithful. The philandering son ran out of money and out of luck, but when he came to his senses, he realized that even as a servant in his father's house he would be better off than as he was, and so he returned. The other brother was not very happy about the outcome.

There are other Gospel stories that echo this same theme: God forgives. No matter the circumstances, no matter our wrong choices, God forgives. That is the promise of hope given by God's covenant with the world.

Depending on whose perspective we take in this story, we will either appreciate God's unlimited love and grace, or we will become annoyed at the fact that someone got to play without ultimately paying. Each person in the story is presented as a complex bundle of emotions and fears.

The father loved both sons, and agreed that there was no need for the younger of the two to await his inheritance. The younger son went off, and the father gave up hope of ever seeing his child again. We know the feeling. Whatever prison has captured whatever we have lost, we fear it will not return, we will never see it again.

The younger son, by now penniless and homeless, had given up hope of forgiveness. How could he return? He may have thought he was taking his part of the inheritance to make his fortune, but he was foolish. So now he is hopelessly embarrassed. He has no claim to the property that will rightfully go to his older brother, if indeed it has not already gone to him. Is his father even still alive? The younger son is imprisoned by his own fears. Somehow, he overcomes them and returns home.

The older son is beyond annoyed. He is downright angry. He has remained at home, toiling in the fields, while his younger brother squandered what he got. The anger is twofold: The older brother is stuck at home. We can be sure he laments his simple status as he envies the freewheeling life he imagines his younger brother has enjoyed. Because this older brother is comparing his life and his own faithfulness to the father's needs with what he assumes has been going on in his brother's life, the knot in his mind hardens into true hatred.

It is a difficult family triangle, almost like a soap opera. How can we understand what Jesus is teaching here?

I think the lesson is one of hope. Hope is central to a life of faith and charity. The father found his lost son, but only because the lost son trusted his father would receive him. The older son does not yet seem to know hope. His father does try to console him: "Everything I have is yours," but there is no affirming "yes" from the older son. If we neglect hope, depression may overtake any of our efforts.

A GRACE FOR TODAY

Lord, help me better learn the virtue of hope.

THIRD SUNDAY OF LENT
Turn It Around

YEAR A: EXODUS 17:3–7; ROMANS 5:1–2, 5–8; JOHN 4:4–52
YEAR B: EXODUS 20:1–17; 1 CORINTHIANS 1:22–25; JOHN 2:13–25
YEAR C: EXODUS 3:1–8A, 13–15; 1 CORINTHIANS 10:1–6, 10–12; LUKE 13:1–9

> The woman said to him, "Sir, give me this water, so that
> I may never be thirsty or have to keep coming here to
> draw water."
>
> John 4:15

E ach reading for the Third Sunday of Lent speaks about conversion. We all have a chance to turn it around. The Samaritan woman, the money changers in the Temple, and the poor barren fig tree remind us of the second chances God freely gives everyone. There is always a new beginning. There is always a chance to grow.

When we look around, outside our lives, we can be pretty critical about what we see. This person did this; that person did that. When someone else comes to us and points out our own faults we might not be very happy about it. But, when you think of it, that person often carries the same message Jesus carried to the Samaritan woman: Take the living water, freely, and be renewed. And, just as Jews and Samaritans were foreigners to each other, sometimes that person may be a total stranger.

Perhaps it is not such a good idea to focus on the indignation of being corrected, especially when there is some (or a lot) of truth to the correction. Perhaps it would be better to focus on the substance offered. It could be the living water Jesus promises.

So also with the money changers in the Temple. Here Jesus is showing his own indignation at the way they act. Some are cheats and some are thieves—much like the tax collectors in other Gospel stories. In any event, they are taking their cut when anyone needs to change foreign coins to pay the Temple tax. The problem is that they are carrying out their business enterprises within the holy place, along with folks selling doves and even livestock.

Jesus has traveled with his disciples to Jerusalem for the Passover, but he is faced with a veritable marketplace inside the Temple. He reacts in anger, but his actions carry the same message: Turn your lives around. Jesus is not condemning commerce here. What he is condemning is mixing up commerce and prayer.

And so with the poor fig tree, which has stood around for too long bearing no fruit. Here Jesus tells about the landowner who complains that every year for three years he has found no fruit on this one fig tree. "Cut it down!" he roars. But his employee, the vineyard keeper says, "Oh, give me a chance. Let me prune it, let me fertilize it, let me care for it, and it will bear fruit."

The fig tree can represent a people, a nation, or a single individual. The point of the story is that there is always a chance to turn it around, to bear fruit. So the fig tree is spared.

We can personalize the messages from each of these three Gospels: We need the cleansing water of life and of forgiveness. We need to clear the clutter from our hearts and minds. We need to accept pruning and nourishment to grow in God's grace and perhaps make a fresh start on the journey.

A GRACE FOR TODAY

Lord, let me accept what I need for conversion.

MONDAY OF THE THIRD WEEK OF LENT
Listening to Prophets
2 KINGS 5:1–15A; LUKE 4:24–30

And he said, "Truly I tell you, no prophet is accepted in
the prophet's hometown...." When they heard this, all in
the synagogue were filled with rage. They got up, drove
him out of the town, and led him to the brow of the hill on
which their town was built, so that they might hurl him
off the cliff. But he passed through the midst of them and
went on his way.

Luke 4:24, 28–30

Things are certainly changing in Jesus's relationship with the people
around him. He gives them examples of earlier prophets—Elijah and
Elisha—who basically could not help the people around them. Only the
very few—the widow in Zarephath in the land of Sidon and Naaman, the
Syrian—were able to hear their preachings and be helped, even healed.

The people's reaction is almost predictable. They nearly run Jesus out of
town. Except that Jesus, the prophet, the Son of God, is so unrecognizable
to them that he passes right through the crowd.

Think of the crowds we have all been in—at a sports match, or in a shop-
ping center, or in a train station or airport. Sometimes there is a smaller

crowd within the larger, disorganized crowd. That smaller crowd is grouped around someone—perhaps a juggler or a preacher—and we cannot quite get close enough to see and hear what is going on. We just know that something is holding the attention of this smaller, somewhat organized group within the larger disorganized and moving mass of people.

Then something happens. Perhaps there is clapping, or a sound of appreciation, or of dismay, and suddenly the crowd dissipates. In an instant what was a group has now melted into the larger moving mass of people, and the center of their attention has shifted back to themselves. And we cannot find the person who drew them together. Somehow he or she has become part of the unidentified crowd.

That is how I see this scene in Luke's Gospel. Jesus was preaching—we have here a record of some of what he must have said—and the people were apparently attentive. Until he crossed them. Until he challenged them. Until he told them that they, like the people who did not hear Elijah or who could not understand Elisha, would not recognize a prophet if he stood before them. Of course he was correct. They did not recognize him.

Such is a deep insult to a crowd of believing Jews, who knew the Scriptures and who honestly did try to live by them. Here is this man, with no credentials (he was not a certified rabbi), with no fixed place to preach, with no status, really, telling them that they could not recognize a prophet in their own day in their own place. As a matter of fact, we have all been there. Often we try to ignore the correcting word when it comes from what we call the "wrong" place. "Who is he?" "Who is she," we ask, "to speak to me or to us in such a matter?" We ignore the correction of the outsider, of the one whose credentials we do not recognize, not because what we hear is incorrect. We ignore that correction because we do not want to know what the person with nothing to lose will say.

Lent is a time to quietly examine our relationships. We examine our relationships with others as well as with the Lord. Too often we want to ignore, even criticize, the ones we come upon who give us the best advice. What "prophet" have you run out of your life lately? And why?

A GRACE FOR TODAY

Lord, let me hear you speaking through others.

TUESDAY OF THE THIRD WEEK OF LENT
Forgiveness
DANIEL 3:25, 34–43; MATTHEW 18:21–35

Then Peter came and said to him, "Lord, if another
member of the church sins against me, how often should
I forgive? As many as seven times?" Jesus said to him,
"Not seven times, but, I tell you, seventy-seven times."

Matthew 18:21–22

Jesus presents a real challenge here. I think the immediate response
many folks have to any "sin against me"—any insult, any falsehood, any
injury—is to write the other person off. That's it. I'm done. Who needs
that one?

Jesus does not agree. The knee-jerk response of writing someone out of
your life is not really the best, and there are many gradations to what Jesus
says to Peter in these simple sentences.

At the first level, Jesus is clearly speaking about someone you know and
whom you know well. Jesus speaks of "your brother." That is about as close
a blood relationship as many people have. Some, of course, do not have
brothers or sisters, but there is usually someone in your life who, except for
familial relationship, really is your brother or your sister. Why do we react
so strongly when one of these "sins" against us? I think we react so strongly

simply because we are so close. We have let the other person uniquely into our lives. We shared sorrows; we shared joys. We shared secrets; we shared hopes. Now, the other has just stepped upon our lives and deeply hurt us.

What to do? Jesus says: Forgive. That is a tall order. We acknowledge the fact that we have deep history with the other, and we recognize the reason we are so hurt and dismayed is that precious history. The choice to walk away and to write the other person off is very painful, yet we naturally want to avoid more pain. But, in writing the other out of our lives we also erase a bit of our own histories. That can be even more painful.

On another level, many others are included in Jesus's advice. There are many others whom we must forgive, but becoming forgiving persons does not mean becoming doormats. Here we must distinguish between forgiving and forgetting. If an acquaintance insults us, we can choose forgiving by finding a reason (he had a bad day, she just lost her job) or we might even forgive without a reason.

Forgetting is a different, and often more difficult choice. If we routinely forget, and then routinely suffer additional indignities, then we must assert our own humanity. But if someone just had a bad day, our own road is easier to walk by just forgetting, whether at work or at school, in the family or at the corner shop. We of course must be alert to those who purposefully hurt us—and we cannot forget about them—but more generally we need to give the other person a chance.

I recall the late archbishop of New York, Cardinal John O'Connor, talking about forgiving and forgetting in relation to the Holocaust. He said we must forgive, but we cannot forget. In his example, what we cannot forget is that people—ordinary human beings—can become so twisted that they can torture and maim and kill other human beings for no reason except that they are Jews, or Gypsies, or Catholic priests and nuns, or any of the others caught in concentration camps.

Still, it is about forgiveness. The bottom line: If we cannot forgive other people, how can we forgive ourselves?

A GRACE FOR TODAY
Lord, let me understand and live forgiveness.

WEDNESDAY OF THE THIRD WEEK OF LENT
Rules
Deuteronomy 4:1, 5–9; Matthew 5:17–19

Do not think that I have come to abolish the law or the prophets; I have come not to abolish but to fulfill.

Matthew 5:17

Some of Jesus's followers thought he intended to change things. But Jesus really did not. Many scholars opine that Jesus did not want to create the new religious belief system the world now recognizes as Christianity, but rather that he intended to reform Judaism in a way that emphasized and retained what was important. His teachings emphasized the meaningful parts of the Law, and gently told his followers—that would now include all Christians—how to live.

Believers today often have the same reaction to prophetic voices as some of the people in Jesus's time. They want to hear what they want to hear, to support their own intentions, and those intentions often include changing things, especially the Law. But Jesus states quite clearly in this passage that the Law and the prophets should neither be abolished nor ignored. Jesus's mission is to fulfill each.

How? Sometimes, I think Jesus's approach to the Law represents a perfect psychology. He gives us an approach we can each follow. Part of what he presents is the application of common sense. In one Gospel, Jesus is shown challenging the men who had gathered to stone the woman caught in adultery (John 8:5–7). His very words move us: Let the one among you who is without sin throw the first stone. Here he does not deny the Law, but he challenges those around him to understand that the punishment is to be to be meted out only by the sinless. Each man recognizes it is not his place—only God's—to judge. Such fulfills the Law as well as the teachings of the prophets.

In other places, Jesus challenges the Law—or bends it a little. He healed on the Sabbath—the man needed the use of his hand (Mark 3:1–6). He chided the Pharisees because they seemed interested in specific regulations about washing yet ignored the commands of God—he specifically cites "Honor your father and your mother" (Matthew 15:1–9). He defended his disciples for picking grain on the Sabbath—they were hungry! (Mark 2:23).

So, what does this say about our own relation to rules, and about our own relation to the prophetic voices around us? First of all, Jesus reminds us about laws. There are boundaries in every part of life. If we ignore those boundaries, if we break the rules, there will be consequences. More important, however, is Jesus's stance that there are rules and then there are rules. He is not saying that rules are made to be broken. What Jesus is saying is that the rule of life can often take precedence over the rules made by people. At an even deeper level, Jesus is teaching us not to be too rigid in our applications of the rules.

As with everything else, Jesus teaches us to live our lives in balance, within the Law, but always listening for his voice as it is echoed in the prophetic voices around us.

A GRACE FOR TODAY

Lord, help me listen to both the Law and the prophets.

THURSDAY OF THE THIRD WEEK OF LENT
Siding with Jesus
JEREMIAH 7:23–28; LUKE 11:14–23

Whoever is not with me is against me, and whoever does
not gather with me scatters.

Luke 11:23

Jesus tells us there are two sets of people in life: those who are with him, and those who are against him. Sometimes the problem is figuring out who's who.

The sad fact is that the world is full of false prophets. They promise the moon, and deliver very little, if anything. Their preaching is rooted in passing fancy, not in Scripture. One particular concern is what is called the "new cosmology," which seems to promise a new way of understanding God and the universe, but which sometimes eliminates the basis for Christianity: the life, death, and resurrection of Jesus the Christ.

There is no way of telling exactly where this new cosmology has come from. Some people say it is an attempt to apply Buddhism, which is a philosophic system and not a religion, to the problem or question of God. Sometimes it seems that some people have added into the mix the writings of others. For example, it seems some people use an admittedly flawed English translation of Teilhard de Chardin's masterful work, *Le Phénomène*

Humain, written in the 1930s and first published in French in 1955 and in English in 1959 as *The Phenomenon of Man.*

Teilhard de Chardin's basic thesis is that the human race is evolving toward a world consciousness whose end, or Omega Point, is a supreme consciousness. Until that time, the world becomes increasingly wrapped in what de Chardin calls a "noosphere of interconnectivity," as technology allows the person to become simultaneously "present" all over the world.

We might think about modern means of communications and the Internet here. The great advances both in interconnectivity and in knowledge at least theoretically can move society to look for a supreme intelligence that created, creates, and coordinates the entire universe. That is one way, actually, of thinking about God (without the electronics, of course.)

But Jesus teaches us a simpler approach to all the advances in technology, in communication, in human thought and in artificial intelligence. Jesus teaches us to use a single objective reality as the touchstone and marker of all our understanding. We approach that touchstone and marker through the Scripture, and we understand that Scripture through the words it gives to Jesus. Without that objective reality, without that touchstone, we might not be able to see clearly what is of God and what is not of God. We might not be able to see clearly who and what is with Jesus and who and what scatters.

A GRACE FOR TODAY

Lord, grant me the wisdom to see things clearly.

FRIDAY OF THE THIRD WEEK OF LENT
Loving
HOSEA 14:2–10; MARK 12:28b–34

One of the scribes came near and heard them disputing with one another, and seeing that he answered them well, he asked him, "Which commandment is the first of all?" Jesus answered, "The first is, 'Hear, O Israel: the Lord our God, the Lord is one; you shall love the Lord your God with all your heart, and with all your soul, and with all your mind, and with all your strength.' The second is this, 'You shall love your neighbor as yourself.' There is no other commandment greater than these."

Mark 12:28b–31

Jesus always has a surprise for those around him. Here, the scribe might be expecting him to roll out the rule book and lay down the law as he, the scribe, might understand it. But Jesus does not. The law he cites is the law of love. Surely the scribes, like many people around Jesus that day, "got it." And, if they did not, we can hope they did eventually.

The simple fact of the matter is: Life is hard. And loving can be harder.

It really can be hard to see things as Jesus does. He tells us we must look at the world and all within it with loving eyes. We need to see as Jesus sees.

And Jesus does not judge; Jesus does not criticize; Jesus does not compete. Jesus loves.

That, I think, is the reason for the worldwide appeal of Pope Francis. It seems the world has fallen in love with him. But he fell in love with the world first! Francis puts on the eyes of love for everyone he meets. Why? And more important perhaps, how?

Go back to the passage for a moment. Jesus cites passages from two books of the Torah: Deuteronomy, the "second Law," and Leviticus, the book explaining rules for priests and the laity. The two passages from these books sum up Jesus's understanding and application of the Law. First, "Love the LORD your God with all your heart, with all your soul, with all your mind, and with all your strength" (Deuteronomy 6:4–5). Second, "Love your neighbor as yourself" (Leviticus 19:18).

When you think of it, these laws of Jesus are not so easy, but neither are they very hard. If we really love God, then we are bound to love God's entire creation. If we love God's entire creation, then we love all in it. If we love all in it, then we love ourselves. If we love ourselves, then we know how to love our neighbor.

There are lots of breaks in that little syllogism. First off, loving a God who is "out there" in space, maybe as a force of light or power that somehow bursts being into the universe, can be pretty easy. I mean, you don't exactly have to sit next to him or her on the subway. Even so, we are told to love this God whom we imagine with our entire hearts, souls, minds, and strength.

So, back to the syllogism. We love God and all creation. That includes the aardvarks, bees, cats, dogs, elephants, and the rest of the menagerie that made it onto Noah's ark. It also includes the fruits and flowers and grass. But the crown of all creation, made in the image and likeness of God, is the human person. That gets us back to the subway, or the classroom, or the workplace. How can we reasonably "love" the next person? Not only that, how can we reasonably love the stranger with our entire hearts, souls, minds, and strength? That is Jesus's second admonition: We must love our neighbors as ourselves.

That is the bottom line. We must love our neighbors as ourselves, but to do so we must love ourselves.

A GRACE FOR TODAY

Lord, let me look at the world—and myself—with loving eyes.

SATURDAY OF THE THIRD WEEK OF LENT
Remembering the Essentials
HOSEA 6:1–6; LUKE 18:9–14

But the tax collector, standing far off, would not even look up to heaven, but was beating his breast and saying, "God, be merciful to me, a sinner!" I tell you, this man went down to his home justified rather than the other; for all who exalt themselves will be humbled, but all who humble themselves will be exalted.

Luke 18:13–14

We can never forget that we are sinners in need of forgiveness. The Gospel passage describing these two people at prayer in the Temple can also describe the two sides of our own personalities. On the one hand, we do follow the rules, and we are glad we are not like the cheats and liars we see around us. On the other hand, we recognize that we are sinners, and often cannot look the Lord in the eye.

The task of the spiritual life is to set things in balance, to be aware of our strengths without turning them into weaknesses. There is nothing worse than the person who is proud of how humble he is. Here, the Pharisee has that sort of silly response to life. He brags about how he follows the Law and earns an honest living. Meanwhile, the poor tax collector knows who he is and what he has done. He has his job, he knows its pitfalls, he knows he is a sinner, and is truly humble before the Lord.

We all have a bit of the Pharisee inside us. We like to think of the good things we have done. Sometimes we even brag about how good we are, at least to others if not to the Lord. That bragging, whether to others or to the Lord, is a bit of an insult to God. It indicates several things: (1) we think we did it all ourselves; (2) we are better than the rest; and, (3) we are pretty insecure. The best approach to the things we might brag about is to take these accomplishments and lay them at the feet of the Lord. Realistically speaking, everything that seems to be yours belongs to God. It is a very good thing to recognize that fact regularly and often.

We also all have a bit of the tax collector inside us. I am not suggesting we have professions we should be ashamed of—although some people genuinely caught in poverty sometimes get involved in some awful things—but we are, each and every single one of us, sinners. That, in and of itself, is a very important recognition to take to heart. Every day in so many ways—in thought and in word and in deed—we have the invitation to sin from within or without, and sometimes we fail.

We can sin in either direction. We can assume we do not need the Lord, or we can think ourselves so unworthy that we end up not respecting God's creation of us with our skills and talents and histories. So, how do we even things up a bit within our own souls?

The task before us, to have a singularly grateful and honest recognition of ourselves and of our lives, cannot be done alone. We need the advice of the people who love us, and we need the ministry of the Church. And we need the humility to accept these.

A GRACE FOR TODAY

Lord, help me to stick to the essentials this Lent.

FOURTH SUNDAY OF LENT
Rejoice!

YEAR A: 1 SAMUEL 16:1B, 6–7, 10–13; EPHESIANS 5:8–14; JOHN 9:1–41
YEAR B: 2 CHRONICLES 36:14–16, 19–23; EPHESIANS 2:4–10; JOHN 3:14–21
YEAR C: JOSHUA 5:9A, 10–12; 2 CORINTHIANS 5:17–21; LUKE 15:1–3, 11–32

> As he walked along, he saw a man blind from birth. …[H]
> e spat on the ground and made mud with the saliva and
> spread the mud on the man's eyes, saying to him, "Go,
> wash in the pool of Siloam" (which means Sent). Then he
> went and washed and came back able to see.
>
> John 9:1, 6–7

Last Thursday marked the midpoint of Lent, and today the Church celebrates Laetare Sunday, a happy day of encouragement in the midst of the long fast. The name comes from the entrance prayer of the Mass, the Introit: "Laetare Jerusalem"—"O be joyful, Jerusalem!"

Today the Church offers a little break in the dense journey of Lent. Other names for this day are just lovely: Mothering Sunday, Refreshment Sunday, and Rose Sunday. The priest and deacon wear rose-colored vestments and each Gospel story for this Sunday brings a swell of joy to our hearts. How must the man blind from birth feel when Jesus, a total stranger, cures his blindness? How must we feel when we hear that God sent his Son not to judge, but to save? And, how do we feel when the Prodigal Son returns to the welcoming arms of his father?

We need each of these passages, and we need each of these feelings, as we take a bit of a Sunday rest from our Lenten fast. Each passage points to the gratuitous gifts of God. Each passage can bring rejoicing deep into our hearts, if we let it.

The blind man knew only that the prophet could cure. There is little more encouraging in life, little that gives more cause for rejoicing, than healing. My own healers—physical and spiritual—touched my ailments and ills and patiently explained their cures. The bottom line was always time. Whether a damaged knee or a damaged psyche, real healing takes time. Sometimes I think we delay rejoicing because, after the cure there are little aftershocks to whatever physical or emotional earthquake damaged us in the first place. Then one day, you just know that there has been a healing and things are repaired. Rejoice!

So also with Jesus's promise that he did not come to judge us. We tend to focus on sin during Lent, sometimes to the point of thinking we've invented a new way to be bad. Yet the Gospel promises that God's Son would save, not judge us, and that he would save the entire world. What a wonderful promise!

We know how much our world needs saving. There are hungry and thirsty people on every continent. They are hungry and thirsty for food and for water, and their poverty also includes needs for education and for political freedom. They suffer the collective sin of the world, but we have God's promise that Jesus would free them. Can we understand that to free them from the pains of their poverty we must cooperate and free ourselves from our own poverties: from lust, gluttony, greed, sloth, anger, envy, and pride? Can we rejoice to know that Jesus does not judge us on our past as we repent of it?

Today is the day for rejoicing, and for understanding the mothering and refreshment God brings to us. Let us rejoice and be glad!

A GRACE FOR TODAY

Lord, let me rejoice always in your love for me.

MONDAY OF THE FOURTH WEEK OF LENT
Healing and Trust
ISAIAH 65:17–21; JOHN 4:43–54

> The official said to him, "Sir, come down before my little
> boy dies." Jesus said to him, "Go; your son will live."
> The man believed the word that Jesus spoke to him and
> started on his way.
>
> John 4:49–50

Can you sense what is going on in the royal official's heart? He is a man of stature and prominence. He has authority over others. Yet here his personal life overtakes whatever embarrassment he might feel at giving way to some other—quite frankly unknown—authority. So he approaches the penniless preacher to ask for a cure.

No matter who we are, it takes a lot to ask for help. There is always that little voice trying to convince you it is all a very dumb idea. "You don't need help," it whispers. "You can do this on your own."

The royal official may have heard that, but he was desperate. His son, perhaps his only son, was ill. So he approaches Jesus and what happens? Jesus does not go with him to his home. Jesus does not lay his hands on him or on his son. Jesus just tells him to go home, his son will live.

Jesus is asking for a huge leap of faith here. The royal official in this Gospel only told Jesus about his son. There are no details. Where was he? Who was he? How far away was he? Jesus seems to be giving him the brush-off, but the royal official believed what Jesus said. He accepted the word of Jesus and, indeed, the end of this Gospel passage reports that the son recovered at the very hour Jesus said his son would live.

Come back to the royal official's dilemma for a moment. He asked for help, and Jesus's response was simply that the help was granted. What did the royal official do? What would you do?

I think sometimes it is easier to listen to those negative whispers and just quit asking. The temptation to quit is always present, but it comes up especially here just beyond the midpoint of the Lenten journey. Discouragement in prayer is a very real temptation. Obviously, if we have been—metaphorically at least—asking for the moon, God is not likely to answer in a way that suits our request. The problem of prayer is well beyond not knowing what to ask for, or how. The problem of prayer is in not believing that God will grant what we need. In fact, if we keep on asking for what we do not need, we will become quite discouraged. I think that is where we need to think about trust.

Of course we ask for all sorts of things: We ask for peace for the friend who just died. We ask for safe travels for the friend on the road. We ask for the health to continue our own journeys. But the attitude with which we approach this prayer—the prayer of petition—must be one of trust. We must trust, we must deeply believe, that God will grant all we need.

The concrete example in today's readings of someone trusting the Lord echoes in our own lives: Jesus has told this man his child will live. How often do we silently hear God's promise, and remain afraid?

A GRACE FOR TODAY

Lord, help me believe you will grant what I need.

TUESDAY OF THE FOURTH WEEK OF LENT
Freedom to Be Healed
Ezekiel 47:1–9, 12; John 5:1–16

One man was there who had been ill for thirty-eight
years. When Jesus saw him lying there and knew that
he had been there a long time, he said to him, "Do you
want to be made well?" The sick man answered him, "Sir,
I have no one to put me into the pool when the water is
stirred up; and while I am making my way, someone else
steps down ahead of me." Jesus said to him, "Stand up,
take your mat and walk."

John 5:5–8

L ent is progressing and the world around Jesus is darkening. He is
healing, here even approaching someone who needs his help. But the
same old problems arise: He healed the lame man on the Sabbath, and the
man then broke the Sabbath himself by picking up his mat and carrying it.

The Jewish rules for the Sabbath are strict and actually very simple.
Today, there are many discussions within the Jewish community about
what is and what is not permitted, but the basic prohibition is work. That
would mean, as it was explained to me once, prohibiting anything that took

place in the building of the Temple—from construction to planting—as well as anything that a person would consider as "work." As I said, Jewish communities today have different ways of looking at the Sabbath restrictions, but if we apply the general idea to Jesus and the man who could not walk, I think we can understand how scandalous Jesus's actions—and those of the man whom he healed—actually were.

First off, the man (unlike the woman with a hemorrhage or the man born blind) did not ask Jesus for help. Jesus approached him. Second, the act of getting up and walking was not prohibited, but the carrying of his mat was.

Now, carrying the mat after being unable to walk after thirty-eight years may not seem strange to us—after all, it may have been one of his sole possessions. But you have to wonder if he really believed what had happened. Was this all true? Could he really walk? I don't think anyone in his circumstance would walk away from his mat. What if the cure did not hold?

Such is a simple problem for anyone healed of anything—of a memory, of a hurt, even of an illness. We want to test things a little, and maybe hang on to the security of the memory or hurt or even illness just a few minutes or even days longer.

It is when we refuse to let go, when we hang on to the memory or hurt, that we really injure ourselves. We let it dig into us more, so that we almost prefer the emotional disfigurement it brings, merely because it is more comfortable to us, and makes us more secure. I think the best example of the refusal to really heal, to let go of a metaphorical mat, came in my life when I was five and broke my elbow. After the cast came off, I needed physical therapy, which consisted of bending my arm, stiff from weeks in the cast. I can tell you quite honestly that I would have preferred to not bend my arm, even to have kept the cast on. The healing and protection created a new kind of hurt, one I had to move through to be really healed.

We all have reasons we cannot be healed, or reasons we will not approach someone and accept the gift of healing. Certainly, Jesus broke the rules by healing on the Sabbath, and the lame man broke the rules by carrying his mat. But we cannot hide behind the "rules" that keep us from progressing, that keep us from being healed.

A GRACE FOR TODAY

Lord, free me to accept your healing touch.

WEDNESDAY OF THE FOURTH WEEK OF LENT
This Is for Real
ISAIAH 49:8–15; JOHN 5:17–30

I can do nothing on my own. As I hear, I judge; and my judgment is just, because I seek to do not my own will but the will of him who sent me.

John 5:30

Jesus's accusers are furious. They have lots of evidence that he ignored the Sabbath prohibitions. Just yesterday we saw that he healed the lame man at the pool. Not only that, the lame man did not approach Jesus, but Jesus approached him. Now Jesus has gone over the top. He is calling God his Father. Think of it: Here is this Jewish preacher, with no real profession, and he is claiming to be the Son of God.

Not only is he claiming to be the Son of God, he is claiming the right—and the ability—to render judgments. This seems to be a different Jesus from the one we knew earlier in Lent, the Jesus who did not render judgment. It is not. Jesus says the dead will hear the voice of the Son of God. Is Jesus here speaking also about the "dead" who refuse to listen to the Word of God, the "dead" who refuse to admit that he, Jesus, is the Son of God? It is they who will be judged, as we know, by their judgment of him!

So Jesus tells those around that he has the power to judge because he is the Son of Man! Jesus makes a huge claim here, but he softens the way it sounds at the end of the passage. He says that no matter what or how he judges, his judgment will be just because he is not seeking to do his own will, but rather the will of the one who sent him. That would be his Father. That would be God.

There is a rumbling in his voice here. Jesus is finally putting forth what the scribes and the Pharisees and the others who tried to trap him want to hear. Jesus is also putting forth his own accusation. Jesus is presenting, fully and openly and honestly, who he is. And he knows full well the consequences. This is for real.

If we look into our own lives we can find ourselves in similar situations. It is important for us to speak the truth and sometimes we must speak the truth to power, but to own up publicly to who we are is an ongoing and often very difficult task.

Are you a Christian? What does that imply? Can you suffer the consequences—socially, economically, even spiritually—of the challenges of Christianity? It is one thing to accept these privately, within the realm of our own personal lives. It is quite something else to live as Jesus did—and to suffer the consequences.

Jesus knows the consequences, but he does not back down. I think all Christians live in the same tension with the world.

A GRACE FOR TODAY
Lord, help me to be in public who I really am.

THURSDAY OF THE FOURTH WEEK OF LENT
Confusion
EXODUS 32:7–14; JOHN 5:31–47

The works that the Father has given me to complete,
the very works that I am doing, testify on my behalf that
the Father has sent me. And the Father who sent me has
himself testified on my behalf. You have never heard
his voice or seen his form, and you do not have his word
abiding in you, because you do not believe him whom he
has sent.

John 5:36–38

The Gospel of John is the fourth of the Gospels. The other three, Matthew, Mark, and Luke, are called the Synoptic Gospels, because they are so similar. But John stands alone as a more philosophical rendering of the truths of Jesus's life. Scholars say it presents what is called a "high Christology," where Jesus is presented as the divine Logos—or Word—through which all is made. Here in this Gospel, Jesus shares his true identity, often only with his disciples.

Parts of the Gospel of John are very confusing. Today, Jesus speaks to the people in a somewhat confusing way about confusion. Whom to believe?

Whom to listen to? Will they listen to Jesus? Will they listen to Scripture?

I think we're all there, listening and a little confused. The clouds of detraction and anger are building around the edges of Jesus's ministry. We know, even though we do not want to know, what will happen to him in the not-too-distant future. Perhaps we want to break into this Gospel story and shout out: Can't you listen? Can't you hear?

Jesus is pretty stern with those around him here. He says, quite clearly, that he came to do what his Father sent him to do, and he is criticized for these actions; they do not believe that the Father sent him because they do not listen to him, the Son; they look through Scripture hoping for eternal life, but ignore its witness to Jesus; and the bottom line is: They do not want to listen to Jesus as the way to eternal life.

But the logical response would be, no, Jesus, I am not listening to you. You break the Law of the Sabbath. Do you not respect the Law? You heal by an unknown power. Do you hold some magic powers? You speak of God as your Father? Do you know that you blaspheme?

Yet, there is so much that is so attractive about Jesus—in fact, these very traits. He has, or at least seems to have, a common sense approach to the Law: If people are hungry they can pick the ears of corn; if people are sick they can be healed. He has, or at least seems to have, the power to heal and he says that God forgives sin. He called God his Father, but he calls me brother or sister. Does that mean that I am a child of God?

These thoughts must have swirled in the minds of the people who saw Jesus in the flesh as he moved around Judea, preaching and teaching, healing and praying. Each positive aspect of what he did had a negative side as well. The result most surely would have been a deep confusion of who he was, of what, exactly, he was teaching.

Does not that happen today? When we hear the words of Scripture, or we hear the words that it attributes to Jesus, can we not find ourselves confused by what is said?

A GRACE FOR TODAY

Lord, help me in my confusion; bring me light.

FRIDAY OF THE FOURTH WEEK OF LENT
Recognizing Christ
WISDOM 2:1A, 12–22; JOHN 7:1–2, 10, 25–30

Now some of the people of Jerusalem were saying, Is not this the man whom they are trying to kill? And here he is, speaking openly, but they say nothing to him! Can it be that the authorities really know that this is the Messiah? Yet we know where this man is from; but when the Messiah comes, no one will know where he is from.

John 7:25–27

The slow march of Lent continues, and the slow, steady beat of anger begins to grow. Jesus is the target. Jesus is the prey. Yet, even as Jesus's time draws near, he continues to speak openly in the Temple. Even though his enemies want to arrest him, he remains free. His time has not yet come.

And so many people still do not recognize him. They question each other: Isn't he the Christ? Isn't he the one they want to kill? And, they answer their own questions: We know who he is, but when he comes no one will recognize him.

Even so, Jesus answers: You know who I am and you know where I am from. The double meanings throw a gauntlet before his enemies as well as before his friends. He is a simple man, and he is from Nazareth, born in Bethlehem. He is also the Son of God, called to redeem all humanity. The paradox is unavoidable: This son of a carpenter who has taught openly in the Temple without ordination or credentials is now claiming, and actually believed by many, to be the Christ.

How much like today. How much like the simplicity of the poor and the lonely, whose eloquent trust explain more about God than all the writings in all the books in the world. I remember driving in El Salvador, back from a visit to Hacienda San Francisco, where the four American women were martyred in 1980. As we turned the bend there was a smiling woman standing behind a long sheet of metal propped over a fire, under a simple lean-to. I asked if it was a roadside stand, perhaps one selling food. No, I was told, it is her kitchen. She lives behind it. What I recall most about that place and that woman was the happiness in her eyes. She was perhaps the poorest person I had ever seen, but the joy she radiated filled the roadside. I think that is when I began to understand—and recognize—the Christ.

So like the people in today's Gospel. I had looked for someone special to teach the finer points of belief. Yet here, before me on a lonely Salvadoran road, was the most basic point of theology: Christ is often invisible because we refuse to recognize him and, we will recognize him if we accept who he is—even when he is within the humble body of a poor woman.

In the Gospel story for today, as Jesus proceeds toward his death, his enemies will not recognize him quite simply because he is the Christ. So much of life goes by them—and us—because we do not clearly understand that fact.

A GRACE FOR TODAY

Lord, help me recognize you.

SATURDAY OF THE FOURTH WEEK OF LENT
Listening and Watching
JEREMIAH 11:18–20; JOHN 7:40–53

Nicodemus, who had gone to Jesus before, and who was one of them, asked, Our law does not judge people without first giving them a hearing to find out what they are doing, does it? They replied, Surely you are not also from Galilee, are you? Search and you will see that no prophet is to arise from Galilee.

John 7:50–52

As Jesus continues to teach, and his enemies are all around him, the discussion turns again to whether he is indeed the Christ. The basic point of disbelief is that this preacher is from Galilee, a mostly rainy, rocky territory that includes Nazareth. That is not what Scripture foretold for the Messiah.

Again the thought comes: What are his credentials? On whose authority does he preach? If he is, indeed, the Christ, the prophet promised from the line of David, then his claims may be true. But who is he, really?

So, even the listeners who might like what he preaches could be convinced that he is guilty of...what? He preaches. He claims to be the Son of God. And he heals, and raises the dead. Surely these last are not magic, or the work of the devil. He seems, overall, to be a good man. Yet he is guilty of claims that even the Jews find difficult.

But, if there is little to prove his innocence, what is there to prove his guilt? Only the outsider in this group, Nicodemus, understands the most basic point: Jesus is innocent of any wrongdoing, and the Law will not allow an innocent person to be condemned. Further, Nicodemus seems to believe that this man truly is the Christ—not only an innocent man, but the innocent Son of God.

No matter. The crowd tells Nicodemus he doesn't know what he is talking about. This man is not the prophet foretold in Scripture. This man is not of the line of David. This man is not the Christ. They are sure of it. They claim: "no prophet arises from Galilee."

So, here is the situation. Jesus's enemies are looking for a way to trap him. He knows this, but he keeps on preaching—openly—to whomever will listen. His claims are real enough for many to believe him. They are also real enough for many to condemn him. People are still listening, but a growing gray cloud of disbelief is starting to overtake them and him. If he was the Christ there would be something else, some other way for them to know for sure. But he is not even from the right territory; he is not from the place that Scripture promised would produce the Christ.

It is maddening. We stare at this scene through our mind's eye and want to shout out: Please, recognize him! Please, know him! Please, understand that he is innocent. Our cries here go unheard perhaps because they are unsaid. And that silence haunts the world today.

There are so many innocent who go unrecognized, who go misunderstood, who go falsely accused, or not accused at all, toward their deaths. We can pick any conflict on any continent and see the same: Some people cry out in defense of the innocent, others cry out to say they cannot be defended—they are from the wrong tribe or nation or race or gender. And, there are very few people, who, like Nicodemus, are willing to take the risk to defend them.

A GRACE FOR TODAY

Lord, grant me the words to defend the innocent.

FIFTH SUNDAY OF LENT
Death Approaches

Year A: Ezekiel 37:12–14; Romans 8:8–11; John 11:1–45
Year B: Jeremiah 31:31–34; Hebrews 5:7–9; John 12:20–33
Year C: Isaiah 43:16–21; Philippians 3:8–14; John 8:1–11

Jesus began to weep.

John 11:35

We fear death, every one of us. Even Jesus in his humanity knew its terror. Perhaps what is most fear-inducing is the prospect of death without redemption, a death actually quite difficult but at least possible to choose.

Each of the Gospels for this final Sunday of Lent brings us to face the realities of our own and others' passions, especially the Passion of Jesus. Jesus wept. He really did. He was fully human and his humanity enveloped a broken heart. Jesus was troubled by the prospect of his Passion, but he knew if he begged to be free of it he would be avoiding his Father's will. Jesus knew the fearfulness of the accused woman, but he condemned neither her nor us. His simple advice: Sin no more.

Lent is indeed a time for prayer and reconciliation, for prayer and reconciliation with ourselves and with our pasts. In many churches during this final week of Lent before Holy Week there will be additional opportunities for confession. Some parishes even hold penance services, where the entire community prays as one for forgiveness before priests—often visitors from other parishes—that offer the opportunity for confession.

So there are really several kinds of death we can think of this day: bodily death, certainly, but also death to sin and sinful acts in light of the death sin brings to our very selves and to our souls. It is all quite frightening. We know nothing of the life beyond. We like to think of it as "life with Christ," but we really do not know what it is or even if it is. Yet the absoluteness and the finality of death approaches us daily, and often comes into our lives with the deaths of those close to us. What is it, beyond an end? We really cannot say.

But we can well understand the notion of the deaths of our souls, if we recognize how we can imprison ourselves through free choices to sin, or become imprisoned through additions to sinful behavior. These chains we can break, and these chains we really should break. But how? Here, many times, we are like Jesus, weeping. Here, many times, we are like Jesus, fearful. Here, many times, we can approach Jesus to ask for forgiveness and encouragement.

Lent offers us the concentrated chance to take a look at the ways and means by which we move further away from life and closer to the death that sin implies. We may weep at our shortcomings, fear we are unable to overcome them, but there is no reason not to listen to Christ's gentle words of encouragement: He does not condemn us, he simply says, "From now on sin no more."

The hope of the resurrection is the beacon in this night. As we daily die to sin and selfishness, we prepare ourselves to rise with Christ at the time of our own natural deaths.

A GRACE FOR TODAY

Lord, quiet my fears.

MONDAY OF THE FIFTH WEEK OF LENT
Throwing Stones
DANIEL 13:1–9, 15–17, 19–30, 33–62; JOHN 8:1–11

Jesus bent down and wrote with his finger on the ground.
When they kept on questioning him, he straightened up
and said to them, "Let anyone among you who is without
sin be the first to throw a stone at her."

John 8:6–7

The scribes and the Pharisees are still trying to trap Jesus. Now they are dragging some poor woman whom they say was "caught in adultery." Notice, they have not brought her accomplice in the supposed crime, nor do they even mention the other person. Their intent is to show that Jesus either follows or does not follow the Law. For all Jesus's preaching about the law of love, here is one case where they are sure he cannot let her go.

They are wrong. Jesus stops the crowd from stoning the woman. His approach is through the law of love, the law that overrides any of our daily accusations and which can inform even the judgments of nation-states. His reasoning here is simple: If you are free of all sin and guilt, go ahead and judge her, go ahead and condemn her, go ahead and stone her to the death she fears.

Jesus's challenge is not necessarily because she is innocent of their claims, although she very well may be. His challenge is because they may be—and most probably are—quite guilty of something.

A telling point in this small story is the fact that the woman's alleged sin is essentially secret. So must be the sins of her accusers. So, in fact, are our own sins. None of us is willing to broadcast our shortcomings. Yet, each of us has them. These may not necessarily be sins—or even sinful inclinations—but whatever they are, they can lead us down the wrong path.

We sin, we are told, in three ways: in thought, in word, in deed. We really sin, essentially, in secret. Only the barest few of us have our actions or our words publicized. None of us has our thoughts revealed. In reality, whether the accused woman sinned or not, only she and God know. In reality, whether we sin or not, really, only we and God know. No one else can judge us. No one else should judge us.

The sinful thoughts that cause us to sin in our actions are well known and understood. We have the Ten Commandments to guide us here. The finer points of the problem of sin have to do with words and thoughts. Too often we do not realize the power of our own words—often because we do not understand how others see us, and therefore do not understand how others feel when one or another of our "words" flies in their direction. Sometimes these words are criticisms. Sometimes these words are judgments. Sometimes these words are opinions. No matter how we couch them, or how we think about them, they are quite possibly not far away from the words and actions of the scribes and the Pharisees.

And, sometimes these words are not let loose from our tongues, but form only in our minds. Here the worst destruction is done. When we develop a critical, judgmental, opinionated way of thinking, about everything and everybody, we find ourselves in a negative and unhappy mental swamp, one that is quite difficult to escape.

A GRACE FOR TODAY

Lord, let me not be negative toward others.

TUESDAY OF THE FIFTH WEEK OF LENT
God Is God
NUMBERS 21:4–9; JOHN 8:21–30

Jesus said, "When you have lifted up the Son of Man, then you will realize that I am he, and that I do nothing on my own, but I speak these things as the Father instructed me. And the one who sent me is with me; he has not left me alone, for I always do what is pleasing to him." As he was saying these things, many believed in him.

John 8:28–30

Jesus is still engaging the Pharisees. They are not on his side, and he well knows it. They would be just as happy to see him out of the picture. Yet he knows exactly what they hope for, and he knows exactly what will happen to him. Even so, he keeps on telling them that he is the Son of God; he is the one who is to come; he is the Christ.

In large part, they couldn't care less. They have made their decisions already. The conflict with Jesus is over the Law and only a few of the Pharisees have come to believe.

But, what do they believe? If we think back over the few Gospel stories in this Lenten season, we will find that Jesus is more than kind and compassionate and nonjudgmental (except perhaps, in the Temple-turned-marketplace). We find Jesus the healer, whose words and actions balm mind and body. These ways of being and these actions suffice for the few who come to believe in this Gospel passage. Jesus clearly is—or at least could be—the Son of God.

And, embedded in the few sentences here attributed to Jesus is a stunning and incredibly encouraging message to us: "He has not left me alone, because I always do what is pleasing to him." Jesus, of course, speaks of God, his—and our—Father. Does it not follow that neither will God leave us alone? Does it not follow that we who do—or at least strive to do—what is pleasing to God will not be left alone? This is God's promise that Jesus passes on to us. Our task is to believe it.

Even so, is not that very aloneness our biggest fear? Is not the fear of being totally alone, without anyone and without any hope, the kind of fear that paralyzes our very hearts and minds? The blackness in that silent void is too much for us to imagine. That is the blackness and the silent void without God. We choose it, freely. Or we do not.

We need not imagine a life without light or hope, a life without God. Here, as Jesus explains that God will not leave him alone he also implicitly promises us that neither will God leave us alone. Jesus promises us that God will not abandon us.

Why? How? We need only the slightest glimmer of light and the faintest warmth of hope to let us see and know our own beautiful creation in God's image. There is no need to fear abandonment by God. There is only the need to fear choosing to abandon God. Meanwhile, as the Psalmist teaches, we must be still, and know that God is God.

A GRACE FOR TODAY

Lord, let me know that God is God.

WEDNESDAY OF THE FIFTH WEEK OF LENT
Children of God
DANIEL 3:14–20, 91–92, 95; JOHN 8:31–42

> They said to him, "We are not illegitimate children; we have one father, God himself." Jesus said to them, "If God were your Father, you would love me, for I came from God and now I am here. I did not come on my own, but he sent me."
>
> John 8:41–42

Jesus restates his quite startling claim today. Here, Jesus is speaking to the Jews who believed in him, who complain: "Our father is Abraham."

He says, quite plainly that he comes from God, he was sent by God, and if those around him understood that God is their Father they would immediately recognize Jesus as his Son. In fact, they and too often we, do not. Jesus's claim still challenges us, even as it challenged—confounded—those who first heard it. Their father is Abraham. Or is he?

Who is your father? The question can raise a complex set of emotions in many people. Some of us have never known our natural fathers, because they died or were out of the picture well before we started looking for them. Others of us do not know or must of necessity question our natural parentage. We may be adopted persons, or IVF children.

However, here Jesus is speaking of a different kind of fatherhood, one that transcends our natural lives. He presents a syllogism: If you knew who God is, then you would know who I am. We can add to that, if we knew who God is, then we would know who we are.

Our natural histories are sacred and special, and each of us has within us the spark of God, the Light that gives light to our souls. That life is a participation in the life of God, and when we recognize that in ourselves we can begin at least to recognize it in others, especially in Jesus. If we are able to see each person before us as part of Christ's participation in the world, we will—I think—begin to understand what Jesus is talking about in this Gospel selection from his life.

Jesus is of God, and if they who are around him understood that they also are children of God then they would love him. They claim to love God. How can they not love Jesus? More important, if they claim to love God, how could they not love themselves?

Such is Jesus's constant challenge. He calls those around him, including us, to understand their and our relationships with him and with his Father. Just as Jesus understands who he is, so we must understand who we are in God: limited, human, and fragile, but also graced, holy, and strong—in God's eyes.

Jesus's followers here persist in thinking of themselves in human terms: Their father is Abraham. Humanly, of course, that is true. None of us can ever deny, nor should we ever decry, our human beginnings, no matter their circumstances. Rather, along with those around Jesus, we must grasp the fullest meaning, the fullest understanding of ourselves as being children of God. Such is Jesus's teaching as he approaches his own death.

A GRACE FOR TODAY

Lord, teach me that I am your beloved child.

The Son of God
GENESIS 17:3–9; JOHN 8:51–59

> Jesus said to them, "Very truly, I tell you, before Abraham
> was, I am." So they picked up stones to throw at him, but
> Jesus hid himself and went out of the temple.
>
> John 8:58–59

As Jesus moves closer to his death, his statements are increasingly scandalous to the people around him. They are beginning to think he is possessed. Not only does he not come from God, but is it possible he is infested with some evil spirit? He simply will not stop claiming that God is his Father.

Now he is speaking again of Abraham, whom the people acknowledge as the natural father of their race. He says he has seen Abraham, whom some scholars say can be placed living around the year 2000 B.C. Abraham has been dead for centuries! So, what is Jesus talking about?

In addition, Jesus applies to himself the same words that God said to Moses: "I AM." (Exodus 3:14). Now Jesus is really confusing his listeners. He claims that he has seen Abraham, by this time long dead, and he repeats the words God spoke to Moses. Jesus says "I AM."

What do these words mean? What does it mean to say "I AM"?

Philosophers and theologians have long pondered God's complete statement, as reported in Exodus: "I AM WHO I AM." They point out that "I AM" means God is a personal God, not an impersonal force of the universe, and that this personal God continually discloses God's unknowable and ineffable self. They further teach that God is a constant and faithful presence, in our personal lives, in the universe as we know it, and even in the universe as we do not know it.

Perhaps among the people listening to Jesus that day there were philosophers who had long thought about the Jewish philosophical notions of the unknowable and ineffable God. How would, how could they react to Jesus's claim? Perhaps among the people that day were scribes and Pharisees who had studied the Scripture and who meditated on the theology of the living God. Surely they would be scandalized by Jesus's claim.

I think if we put ourselves in their sandals we can think the same. The God whom we cannot name (because the name would contain God, who is limitless) is the God whom we cannot know (because to know is to understand). The God who is, is. Knowledge of God cannot be contained by a person, because to be contained is to be limited, and to be a person is to be knowable.

Such is the paradox of Jesus the Christ in the world. Because God is limitless he assumed human form and lived a limited life. Because God is unknowable, he became a person whom we can know. Jesus is God's gift of God's self to space and time precisely so we can come slightly closer to understanding God and to understanding ourselves in relation to God.

And, as all this is unfolding, we again stare in amazement that what Jesus knew—his time had not yet come—is true. They pick up stones to throw at him but he hides himself, and escapes.

How true this is of our own lives. We are like the people: We do not understand, and when we do understand we cannot believe. And because we cannot believe we seek to end the cause of our confusion.

Jesus can run away from his accusers, but there is no running away from the fact of God's revelation in him and in his life and teachings. No matter how the world tries to end him and them, it is unsuccessful. Surely, this is a power of the Son of God.

A GRACE FOR TODAY

Lord, help me understand you and your Father.

FRIDAY OF THE FIFTH WEEK OF LENT
Works of the Father
JEREMIAH 20:10–13; JOHN 10:31–42

If I am not doing the works of my Father, then do not
believe me. But if I do them, even though you do not
believe me, believe the works, so that you may know and
understand that the Father is in me and I am in the Father.

John 10:37–38

A gain they pick up rocks to stone Jesus. Again he escapes. His defense
to their charge is simple: Either he performs the Father's works or he
does not. Believe or disbelieve according to those terms.

Jesus also presents a very interesting challenge within his defense. Even
if you do not believe him, believe his works. That is, his works are so
connected to his belief in the Father, and in himself, that the works alone
should logically lead to believing in him as well as in the Father.

How do we face Jesus's challenge? We know in our deepest selves that
there is more to life than what we see and hear and smell and touch and
taste. These senses are, realistically speaking, the only ways we can perceive
what is, yet, no matter how hard we try to understand God, we can only
approach the unknown and uncreated reality of God through God's works.

In the largest sense, these works are everything within and about us, within and about the world. These we know through our senses.

So, we see the moon and the sun, we hear the birds and the crashing waves, we smell fresh air and flowers. We touch each other and the beings and things around us, and we taste food and drink. We find, if not directly then indirectly, the hand of God in all creation, and we come to realize, sometimes very slowly, that we are a part of it all. We are a part of God's works, we are a part of God's creation.

Jesus here, of course, is speaking of his works of teaching and feeding and healing—all somewhat miraculous. How could he know the Scriptures so well? How could he feed the many who listened to him? How could he heal the sick, even raise the dead? These works, he says, are not his, but the works of the Father who sent him. Is there another explanation?

I think it is fairly logical for those who are collecting the stones to kill Jesus to react as they do, mainly because he is challenging not only authority but the authority of the Law. Who is he to teach? Who is he to feed strangers without the proper rituals? Who is he to heal and raise the dead, even on the Sabbath? While we may look at his accusers hanging on to the particulars of the Law in order to rid themselves of this Jesus, we need to remember that even this teaching contains what they complain about. That is, it is not what he says so much as what he does. And, what he does is point to the Father, always.

The Law can tend to complicate matters. Common sense tends to point to God's actions. We follow Jesus in trying to understand Scripture. We follow Jesus in sharing our goods. We follow Jesus in trying to help where we can. The simple folk across the Jordan believe in Jesus. Even as his time approaches, can we?

A GRACE FOR TODAY

Lord, let me believe in you and your works.

SATURDAY OF THE FIFTH WEEK OF LENT

Hidden in Jesus's Anguish

EZEKIEL 37:21–28; JOHN 11:45–56

So from that day on they planned to put him to death.

Jesus therefore no longer walked about openly among
the Jews, but went from there to a town called Ephraim
in the region near the wilderness; and he remained there
with the disciples.

John 11:53–54

Here is the situation: Many of the Jews—they who had come to Mary Magdalene—believe in Jesus. Many others do not, and so they go to the Pharisees to report Jesus's words and actions. Caiaphas, the high priest that year, is in a delicate situation with the Roman government. His interests, however, are strictly political: Jesus troubles the delicate balance of power in Jerusalem. The Jews and the Roman government have been coexisting peacefully, if not happily. Now this traveling preacher threatens things. He is upsetting the Jews and the festival of Passover is approaching. Above all, Caiaphas wants to keep the peace.

Meanwhile, Jesus knows his situation—and his enemies—all too well. He has left Jerusalem for the desert lands and a town called Ephraim. He should come back to Jerusalem for the Passover. Will he?

Of course we know in advance that he will, and we know in advance what will happen. But as we watch the events of Jesus's final days unfold, we cannot help but wonder if things could have been different. Could he have stayed away? Could Caiaphas have determined that he was not such a threat after all? Could anything have changed?

Such is the frustration that rises within us when we see and hear the chief priest discussing Jesus as a threat to the political balance in Jerusalem and in the region. How like today! So many situations, large and small, catch our eye as we think about Jesus's plight here, and the reactions of the believers, of the unbeliever, and of the authorities.

History recounts thousands of similar situations. A single individual, or a small group of people, see an injustice. They teach, they feed, they heal the storms of division within a given political system, be it a private group or a nation-state. Whom can we name? Martin Luther King, Jr., in the United States. Nelson Mandela, in South Africa. Mother Teresa, in India and around the world. These are the beacons of God's light in many darknesses, and there are hundreds and thousands of other individuals who are like them.

The ones we know about and the ones we do not know about and their followers felt Jesus's anguish over the poor and disenfranchised of their own and others' societies and they did something about it. Yes, Jesus escaped to a town called Ephraim. That name means "double fruitfulness."

Most of us are unable to do the same. Many of us can do a little. All of us can do something.

A GRACE FOR TODAY

Lord, let me sense your anguish so I may know it in your people.

PALM SUNDAY OF THE LORD'S PASSION
Holy Week Begins

Opening Proclamation: Year A: Matthew 21:1-11; Year B: Mark
11:1-10 or John 16: Year C: Luke 19:28-40.
First Reading and Second Reading, Years A, B, C: Isaiah 50:4–7;
Philippians 2:6–11.
Gospel: Year A: Matthew 26:14—27:66; Year B: Mark 14:1—
15:47; Year C: Luke 22:14—23:56

> Those who went ahead and those who followed were
> shouting, Hosanna!
> Blessed is the one who comes in the name of the Lord!
> Blessed is the coming kingdom of our ancestor David!
> Hosanna in the highest heaven!
>
> Mark 11:9–10

The Mass for Palm, or Passion, Sunday begins with either a solemn
or simple entrance. In most churches, the main Mass includes the
solemn entrance, and the people process waving palms, as in one of the
three Gospel accounts of Jesus's return to Jerusalem read at the start of the
ceremonies.

The reading of the Passion according to St. Matthew is reserved for the Mass on Palm Sunday. Typically three readers and the congregation as a whole will speak the parts: narrator, voices, Christ, crowd. The action of the Mass encompasses all the events of Holy Week, including the Crucifixion.

On Palm Sunday, some churches have an afternoon concert of Johann Sebastian Bach's baroque masterpiece, *Passio Domini Nostri J.C. Secundum Evangelistam Matthaeum.* The Passion is near, but the focus of Palm Sunday is Jesus's triumphal return to Jerusalem, riding on a simple beast. His followers celebrate him; he is hailed as "King of the Jews." There is excitement in the air, and for a moment perhaps he—and we—can forget the Passion that lies ahead.

But that moment is all too fleeting. We all know this feeling. There are times in our lives when we cannot believe what is ahead, because we see nothing but darkness and sadness and strife. Often, these surround us, either in reality or in our minds. No matter whether they are embedded in our own lives or in the lives of others, they begin to close in, to choke the life out of our hopes and dreams.

Sometimes this is because we think we have to do "it" all on our own. Often the choking darkness, sadness, and strife belong to our personal lives: Our careers have gone sour, or are ending; our family and friends have deserted us, or died; our health is waning or completely failing. Many times the grinding negatives belong to our worldviews: poverty, political corruption, and all the other markers of evil float in our minds and cause us deep sorrow and pain. Parts of our responses are totally human and normal, but other parts can be beyond these. In our own passions, we need to respect ourselves and respect what, exactly, we can do as fragile human beings.

Jesus's Passion is terrifying, and so are ours. Yet, our faith—and Scripture—tell us that Jesus remained aware of the Father. Did he doubt? Probably. Did he allow his doubts to overcome him? We can argue both sides of the story, and see in Jesus's Passion our own.

If we return, however, to Jesus's coming in triumph to Jerusalem, we must recall that his triumph is in the Gospel. The good news of his preaching is a joyful reformation of the Law to a law that regulates but does not damage the spirit. This is the Jesus who taught and healed. He claims to be the Son of God, and he promises everlasting life for all. At the very moment he enters Jerusalem, he seems unstoppable.

A GRACE FOR TODAY

Lord, let me continually welcome you.

MONDAY OF HOLY WEEK
Preparing for Death
ISAIAH 42:1–7; JOHN 12:1–11

Mary took a pound of costly perfume made of pure nard, anointed Jesus' feet, and wiped them with her hair. The house was filled with the fragrance of the perfume.

John 12:3

Today's Gospel returns us to Bethany, where Mary, Martha, and their raised brother Lazarus live. Here, six days before the Passover they gather for another festive event, quite probably a Friday night dinner beginning the Sabbath, for Jesus and the disciples. It is the Jewish tradition to walk, not ride, during the Sabbath, and the visitors would have washed their feet upon arriving at the siblings' home.

We see Mary take the precious oil usually used for burial preparations and pour it on Jesus's feet. So many words and themes from Scripture come to mind. Jesus is the Anointed One. We know he is God's Chosen One. Mary anoints him, and we recall the anointing of healing and forgiveness.

Judas complains. The oil should have been sold and the money given to the poor. Jesus's comment resounds in our minds and hearts: "You always have the poor with you, but you do not always have me" (John 12:8).

True enough, in this scene and in our lives today. They who are poor in so many ways cry out for our help: for material needs, for spiritual needs, and simply for attention. More than any human suffering possible the fact of being unknown, uncelebrated, uncared for is the deepest hurt. Here Jesus teaches us, as he attempts to explain to Judas, that material things are not all that important. Of course, we cannot ignore the hungry or the homeless, but the more general need, even of these, is to be paid attention to, to be celebrated.

Our time and our talents are what we have to share, what we have to present to those around us. These are the oils of healing that we can squander on the ailments of real persons around us. I think sometimes we take others for granted. We know about, but perhaps do not cherish, the presence of our friends and family. Yet we can hear Jesus's words coming from them: "You do not always have me." And, we will not always have them. Relationships end. People move away. They die.

Mary here is preparing for the death of Jesus, symbolically preparing him, but also preparing herself. She pours the precious oil on him. I think we can do the same within all our relationships. We will not always have them among us. We will lose them, every single one of them, in one way or another. So the time for "preparation" for the burial is now: We celebrate with festive meals, we "anoint" them in whatever ways we can. We share our very selves with them and we encourage them, as well as ourselves, to know and to believe that they and we are God's special creations.

The voice of Judas that whispers in the back of our minds and memories wants to turn us away from that celebration with the most slippery of "good" reasons: Save the money.

Here during Holy Week we recognize how close is the death of Jesus. Do we recognize how close are our own deaths, and the deaths of those whom we love?

A GRACE FOR TODAY

Lord, help me do something soon for one I love.

TUESDAY OF HOLY WEEK
Betrayal, Denial, Confusion
ISAIAH 49:1–6; JOHN: 13:21–33, 36–38

Simon Peter said to him, "Lord, where are you going?" Jesus answered, "Where I am going, you cannot follow me now; but you will follow afterward." Peter said to him, "Lord, why can I not follow you now? I will lay down my life for you." Jesus answered, "Will you lay down your life for me? Very truly, I tell you, before the cock crows, you will have denied me three times."

John 13:36–38

Jesus's friends are still with him this night. No matter how many times we read or hear the story, it always comes out the same. Jesus says there is a betrayer among them: It is Judas. Judas takes the small bit of food Jesus gives him to eat and leaves the gathering. The others kindly assume Judas has gone to buy food for the poor.

Peter says he will never betray Jesus. He clearly believes what he says. We know, of course, what is coming. Jesus predicts Peter will deny him three times before the cock crows to greet the dawn. Yet Jesus does not condemn Peter.

These two predictions, of betrayal and denial, are the backdrop against which the others hear Jesus say he is leaving and that they cannot go with him. Here Jesus speaks in a difficult, even confusing manner: "Now the Son of Man has been glorified, and God has been glorified in him. If God has been glorified in him, God will also glorify him in himself and will glorify him at once" (John 13:31–32).

Jesus's statement here is the center of the historical Passion, and the disclosure of Jesus's heart as the true child of the Father. Jesus's statement here encompasses the history of his life and predicts both his death and immediate resurrection. As God is glorified in Jesus, so God glorifies Jesus in Godself, and God will glorify him, that is, bring Jesus to God's own light and life *at once.*

When Jesus directly applies God's actions to the disciples, we hear the heartening promise that even though they cannot follow Jesus immediately, they will assuredly follow him later to this glory. Peter seems to get it. He knows the forces around Jesus are darkening. He asks Jesus why he cannot follow him right then, it would seem to the Crucifixion they all know is coming, but perhaps which is too terrible to speak or even think about. Peter promises he will lay down his life for Jesus. Here Jesus predicts Peter's denial.

How like them are we all. We see Jesus betrayed and denied all around us. We even, at some level (no matter how minor) betray and deny Jesus often. The larger betrayals and denials are awful to behold: Children's lives are damaged and destroyed in so many ways; mass murder crosses our paths through war and through lunacy; corporations and governments rob individuals of their land and money. These awful acts outside ourselves betray the living Christ in the world, and they continue even when they are exposed.

The smaller betrayals in our own lives are dangerously like the large ones. With anger we "kill" a friendship or a reputation; with greed we "steal" from others by being miserly with time or possessions. These minor (or sometimes major) free acts of ours betray the living Christ within us and within other persons. These smaller contributions to the anguish of the world are our own denials of Christ within and without.

A GRACE FOR TODAY
Lord, show me how I betray and deny you.

WEDNESDAY OF HOLY WEEK
Spy Wednesday
Isaiah 50:4–9a; Matthew 26:14–25

> While they were eating, he said, "Truly I tell you, one of you will betray me." And they became greatly distressed and began to say to him one after another, "Surely not I, Lord?" He answered, "The one who has dipped his hand into the bowl with me will betray me."
>
> Matthew 26:21–23

Today, often called "Spy Wednesday," again recounts Judas's betrayal of Jesus. The scene is terrible. Judas has come from selling out Jesus, from agreeing to point Jesus out to the authorities who come to arrest him. Judas holds in his purse his payment for the betrayal: thirty pieces of silver. He has betrayed his teacher, yet he still eats with him. How awful.

When we look into the Gospels of Jesus's life, we can certainly see the horror of Judas's actions. The initial act, selling information, is bad enough, but like so many betrayers Judas both covers and compounds his act by eating the Passover supper with the other disciples. They are gathered and sheltered from the political storm brewing about them. They sense the sadness in Jesus, and with astonishment hear his announcement that one among them would betray him.

How did he know? How did Jesus know that Judas sat at table with the price of his life, with thirty pieces of silver? The others stare in anguished awe, asking, "Surely not I, Lord?" (Matthew 26:22).

We all have that feeling. We all know in our private lives and in our public, political lives as well, that we are liable to betray the Lord. We know the metaphorical "trick knees" in our histories that can bring us today to betray ourselves as fully human creatures of God, which can bring us to some sinful betrayal of our beliefs. One by one the disciples ask Jesus: Is it I?

Jesus calms their individual fears a little, at least for now. The one who dipped his hand into the dish with Jesus will betray him. Jesus knows it is Judas, we know it is Judas, now the others know as well that Judas will ignite the torch to light the way for the authorities to arrest Jesus. It is a terrifying moment. One of Jesus's closest followers, in fact the one entrusted with the small band's money, is so engaged with funds and so distracted from the realities of Jesus's life and teachings, that he has sold his master's life for a pittance.

Jesus predicts Judas's despair. In so doing, Jesus predicts our own despair when we turn away from him and from the Father. There are three internal storms here, and each can shed light on how we move through this final day of Lent and beyond. First: Each disciple is confused and frightened at the prospect of betraying the Lord. Second: Jesus is devastated by the betrayal. Third: Judas is troubled and will become more disturbed by his action.

We have these same reactions when sin presents itself to us as an attractive option. If our hearts are calm, we will become confused and frightened at the possibilities presented to us—evil so often masquerades as some good. Here it is Judas's reputation with the authorities and his personal profit. If we do fall, and place our actions before Christ, we can recognize how we have hurt him—because as members of his body everything we do affects every other of us. And, as we recognize the damage we have done to ourselves and to the body of Christ, we become more and more sorrowful.

I do not mean to say that every sin will cause us to consider suicide. I do say that every sin moves us, each and all, further away from life in Christ.

A GRACE FOR TODAY

Lord, help me understand the nature of sin.

HOLY THURSDAY
This Is My Body
EXODUS 12:1–8, 11–14; 1 CORINTHIANS 11:23–26; JOHN 13:1–15

> Peter said to him, "You will never wash my feet." Jesus answered, "Unless I wash you, you have no share with me." Simon Peter said to him, "Lord, not my feet only but also my hands and my head!"
>
> John 13:8–9

The Holy Thursday liturgy focuses on the body of Christ. The washed feet belong to the body of Christ. The blessed bread actually becomes the Body of Christ. It is offered to all with the simple words: "The Body of Christ." We not only receive the Body of Christ; we are called the body of Christ.

The Gospel focuses on Jesus's actions at what has come to be called the Last Supper. Jesus knows exactly who he is, and where his future lies. His relatively distant future is of eternal life with the Father. His near future is one of suffering, dejection, fear, anguish, pain, abandonment, and the invitation to despair. What does he do? He kneels before the disciples and washes their feet.

Peter objects, as well we might. Who is he—who am I—that my Lord will kneel before me? Jesus explains that if he will not receive Jesus's ministry in this way, then he will have rejected Jesus. So good old Peter says, yes—wash all of me! But Jesus, knowing Peter is a good man, says there is no need to ask for that. Only his feet need washing.

What does Jesus's service mean? What does the foot-washing signify? Some commentators notice that it is Pope Francis's custom to wear a diaconal stole while participating in the Holy Thursday foot-washing ceremonies of both men and women. Since the Middle Ages, priests were first ordained as deacons before they received priestly ordination, but in the early church there were specific duties for the separate orders of priests and deacons.

Today the Church recognizes that the priest and bishop, on the one hand, represent Jesus as the head of the Church; whereas the deacon represents Jesus as servant. Every bishop knows he carries within him the fullness of these orders—each even wears the diaconal dalmatic beneath his chasuble in significant ceremonies—and so Francis wears the stole of a deacon when he washes the feet of the people—male and female—who represent the larger body of disciples and they who hear Jesus's message.

To wash the feet of men and women takes the focus away from any thought that the people whose feet are washed are only the apostles and moves the focus to the larger body of disciples. So the focus of the ceremonial foot-washing becomes the ministry of service, one of the three charges of the deacon. Liturgical spats aside, when the ceremony includes a broad representation of the people, it represents the broad reach of Jesus's healing, cleansing, ministry.

The center of Jesus's ministry is his Gospel, and the center of diaconal life is carrying the Gospel. The deacon carries the Gospel ceremonially in the liturgy; the deacon carries the Gospel actually in life by ministry—whether the metaphorical ministry of foot-washing or the real ministry of charity.

We are all called to service. We are all called to be part of the body of Christ.

A GRACE FOR TODAY

Lord, let me be the Christ I receive.

This Is My Blood

ISAIAH 52:13—53:12; HEBREWS 4:14–16; 5:7–9; JOHN 18:1—19:42

> After this, when Jesus knew that all was now finished,
> he said (in order to fulfill the scripture), "I am thirsty."
> A jar full of sour wine was standing there. So they put a
> sponge full of the wine on a branch of hyssop and held
> it to his mouth. When Jesus had received the wine, he
> said, "It is finished." Then he bowed his head and gave
> up his spirit.
>
> John 19:28–30

No matter how often we hear the events surrounding the Crucifixion of Jesus retold, we cannot believe them. Different Gospels portray him slightly differently—the "seven last words" are compiled from the four Gospels. In Matthew and Mark we hear Jesus cry out in anguish: "My God, why have you forsaken me?" (Matthew 27:46; Mark 15:34).

In Luke's Gospel, Jesus asks his Father to forgive those who crucify him (Luke 23:34); promises the "good thief" he will be with him in paradise (Luke 23:43); and says, "Father, into your hands I commend my spirit" (Luke 23:46). In John's Gospel, read today, Jesus commends his mother to

John (John 19:26–27); he says, "I am thirsty" (John 19:28); and then soon says, "It is finished." (John 19:30).

What are we to make of these words? What are we to make of the entire story? Some critics argue that the differing reports of the Crucifixion prove that the story is made up. They neglect to point out that accounts of any event differ in their retelling by different people. They also neglect the accounts of Jesus's life and death from other than Christian sources.

John's account comes toward the end of his difficult Gospel, a Gospel that emphasizes Jesus's divinity. As we re-read John's account from year to year, we may find ourselves among the doubters, perhaps influenced by the secular assaults on all belief systems.

If we place ourselves among the doubters watching the scene, perhaps we can feel what they felt. He claims to be the Son of God, and he had many disciples, yet his followers are not all here. He seems frightened, and he is bleeding and gasping for breath just like any other man. He is no different from the other criminals.

If we place ourselves among the believers watching the scene, we can sense his loving care for his mother, and his belief in John's friendship. We have an awful tug when he whispers of his thirst. We weep inside and out when he says, "It is finished."

Or, maybe we can place ourselves among the "in-betweens"—they who want to believe, who hope to believe, but who are just not exactly sure about what is going on.

I think we are each in all three of these categories: doubters, believers, and in-betweens at one stage or another throughout the Passion, and throughout our lives. Jesus's story is really a very confusing and ultimately sad story. He went about doing good—teaching, preaching, healing, consoling—but even one of his own closest disciples betrayed him.

It is impossible not to think of our own lives here. The psychological pain Jesus suffers at this drastic turn of events must be somewhat like our own in tragedy. The physical pain must be awful, and if we have not suffered severe pain, we surely know others who have. And, beyond these, there is the question that must have crossed his mind: Is this real? Am I going to rise?

That is our own ultimate question.

A GRACE FOR TODAY

Lord, grant me compassion for myself and others in our doubts and fears.

HOLY SATURDAY
Hope and Fear

There is no Mass proper to Holy Saturday. It is a day of quiet waiting. An ancient homily for today says, "The whole earth keeps silence because the King is asleep." Such is the truth. Such is the fear. Such is the hope.

Jesus really died. He died and he died for us and the whole earth rumbled. Now the earth—and we—are silent. The challenge is to recognize our fear today. We are human. We will die. We do not know what will happen after that. But we also know that Jesus was human. Jesus died. And, he rose from the dead. Too often we forget that fact.

Where is Jesus now? Where is Jesus on this Holy Saturday as we hope for the Easter dawn? Where is Jesus in all the other Holy Saturdays of our lives?

There is a deep need within our societies and our personal psyches for hope. Yet, even as we acknowledge our communal and individual needs for hope, we reject it even as it is offered gratuitously to us. Sure, we say, Easter will come. Jesus will rise. But do we really know that? Do we really believe that?

Sometimes I think we breeze through Holy Saturday as just another day—this one "off" from the usual liturgies—just a day to do something else now that Lent has ended. But Holy Saturday is the one day when we can hold our entire lives in balance. We have seen the Crucifixion of Jesus. He died. He was buried. What will be next?

The key to this day is hope. Without hope we discount our humanity as children of God. Without hope we will be unable to know that Jesus rose for us personally and really. Without the hope of Holy Saturday we will not see the dawn of Easter.

A GRACE FOR TODAY
Lord, help me live in hope.

EASTER SUNDAY
The Tomb Is Empty: Rejoice!
Acts 10:34a, 37–43; Colossians 3:1–4 or 1 Corinthians 5:6b–8;
John 20:1–9

> Early on the first day of the week, while it was still dark,
> Mary Magdalene came to the tomb and saw that the stone
> had been removed from the tomb. So she ran and went to
> Simon Peter and the other disciple, the one whom Jesus
> loved, and said to them, "They have taken the Lord out of
> the tomb, and we do not know where they have laid him."
>
> John 20:1–2

Holy Saturday, the day of quiet waiting, has passed. The first three stars shine on the quiet tomb. The Sabbath has ended.

Each of the four Gospels tells the same story: Mary Magdalene and the other women found the tomb empty, and announced the resurrection to the apostles. From Gospel to Gospel the names and number of women change slightly, but Mary Magdalene is always there.

At first they are perplexed, even afraid. They go to the tomb and the stone is rolled away. Jesus's body is not there. Almost every depiction of this first Easter morn has the women startled, perhaps fearful. Holy Saturday has turned to Sunday morning and the hope that waited silently is arising in their hearts. Soon Mary Magdalene's excited testimony convinces the men to come and see for themselves: The tomb is empty.

Mary Magdalene's name has been clouded by history and the telling of Jesus's actual appearance to her comes only in Easter Vigil, but not on Easter Sunday. However, there is no rewriting history. It is quite clear that Jesus first revealed himself to her, that the glory of God revealed in him shone first on her, that the promise of resurrection now living in him burst into her history before any other's.

As Easter opens up the season of rejoicing, we may find the resurrection has not yet entered our hearts. Where is the bouncing happiness? Where is the whirling joy? I sometimes think there is a simplicity to the resurrection that we can too easily overlook. God is real. God has entered into history, into your life, into my life, through the life, death, and resurrection of Jesus, who remains with you and with me, personally, to the end of time.

There is a stillness to the heart and the mind when we recognize that fact and cherish it. He is risen. He is risen indeed!

A GRACE FOR TODAY

Lord, help me live your resurrection.

ABOUT THE AUTHOR

Phyllis Zagano is an internationally acclaimed Catholic scholar and lecturer on contemporary spirituality and women's issues in the Church. Previous books include *Women Deacons: Past, Present, Future* (with Gary Macy and William T. Ditewig), *Mysticism and the Spiritual Quest,* and *On Prayer: A Letter for My Godchild.* Her twice-monthly column, *Just Catholic,* runs in the *National Catholic Reporter.*